REINVENT **YOUR** RELATIONSHIP

REINVENT **YOUR** RELATIONSHIP

*A Therapist's Insights to
Having the Relationship
You've Always Wanted*

Ana Aluisy
LMHC, LMFT

New York

REINVENT **YOUR** RELATIONSHIP

A Therapist's Insights to Having the Relationship You've Always Wanted

© 2016 Ana Aluisy, LMHC, LMFT.

Published in New York, New York, by Morgan James Publishing. Morgan James and The Entrepreneurial Publisher are trademarks of Morgan James, LLC.
www.MorganJamesPublishing.com

The Morgan James Speakers Group can bring authors to your live event. For more information or to book an event visit The Morgan James Speakers Group at www.TheMorganJamesSpeakersGroup.com.

Shelfie

A **free** eBook edition is available
with the purchase of this print book.

CLEARLY PRINT YOUR NAME ABOVE IN UPPER CASE

Instructions to claim your free eBook edition:
1. Download the Shelfie app for Android or iOS
2. Write your name in **UPPER CASE** above
3. Use the Shelfie app to submit a photo
4. Download your eBook to any device

ISBN 978-1-63047-895-7 paperback
ISBN 978-1-63047-896-4 eBook
ISBN 978-1-63047-897-1 hardcover
Library of Congress Control Number:
2015919619

Cover Design by:
Gabriel Alusiy

Interior Design by:
Bonnie Bushman
The Whole Caboodle Graphic Design

In an effort to support local communities and raise awareness and funds, Morgan James Publishing donates a percentage of all book sales for the life of each book to Habitat for Humanity Peninsula and Greater Williamsburg.

Get involved today, visit
www.MorganJamesBuilds.com

Habitat
for Humanity®
Peninsula and
Greater Williamsburg
Building Partner

For Lucas and Marco

TABLE OF CONTENTS

ACKNOWLEDGMENTS

This book could not have been written without the support and guidance of family, friends, and colleagues who encouraged me and supported me throughout. I want to thank my incredible husband Gabriel for his guidance and support while I wrote this book. Thank you for pushing me and inspiring me everyday. My mother, Zaida, for teaching me the values that shape me today and being there for me when I need it. My father, Luis, for expressing his support and encouragement. My siblings, Lili, Coco, and Mico, for your unconditional encouragement and being my partners in crime since childhood. My professors, Dr. Tennyson Wright, Dr. Ryan Henry, and Dr. Gary DuDell, who believed in me when I didn't know how to and helped shaped the professional that I am today. The team at Entrevo USA and KPI Tampa for guiding me and keeping me accountable.

INTRODUCTION

Mitch and Gina sit on a couch, snuggled close together. Mitch scrolls through movies on Netflix, while Gina fiddles with her phone, looking for delivery. It's a pleasant moment shared together at home—a rare quiet, relaxed evening in their typically busy and bustling lives. Relaxed, that is, until the dreaded question materializes...

"So what do you want to order for dinner?"

"Doesn't matter to me, babe. Whatever you want works."

"OK, in that case let's get Thai food."

"Ugh! Anything BUT Thai food."

"Well, then you should have SAID 'whatever you want works, EXCEPT Thai food.' Gina sits up, pulling away from Mitch, clearly irritated. Mitch sighs--a little too loudly, and Gina definitely notices this. Suddenly the body language of the couple shifts, becoming defensive. The mood darkens. The tension in the room grows.

"I'm sorry, it's just that we had that for lunch today at the office."

"Well, I can't be expected to know that. How about the new Italian place?"

"OK, sure, whatever. What do you feel like watching? Oooh, they just added *Saving Private Ryan!*"

"What's wrong with you? That movie is a bloodbath, I don't want to watch that while I'm eating!"

"Oh come on, it's a classic movie! It's practically an art film. It's not like I want to watch *Rambo*." Gina rolls her eyes.

"Hey, don't roll your eyes at me! God, you ALWAYS do this."

"Do what? You have no sense of what is appropriate. You wanted to watch a shoot-em-up movie on our honeymoon, for god's sake!"

"Are you EVER going to let that go? Christ, it was YEARS ago, get over it already!"

"Don't tell me how to feel!"

Does this scene seem familiar? Arguments in relationships are common, but often times our ideas, opinions, and desires can be misunderstood. The previous dialogue between Mitch and Gina goes beyond food and movies. They both want to spend time together, but their limited communication, lack of validation, and disappointments from the past get in the way of enjoying time together.

If you're an adult in a relationship with a significant other and are interested in repairing or simply improving your relationship, picking up this book can be the first step to a brighter future. As an adult in a loving relationship as well as a couples' therapist, I know that we all need help when it comes to solving difficulties and disagreements in our relationship.

Relationships can seem easy and smooth in the beginning. This stage of a relationship only lasts the time necessary to meet a partner and obtain more information about their values, rituals, and priorities. You may find that this person is so special to you that you'll be willing to adapt to his or her ways, or you may grow so annoyed or frustrated that you even question the feelings you may have for them. Either way, all relationships have problems. It's a normal part of life to have differences that can result in conflict. It's our ability to deal with these conflicts or differences that are going to help us be successful (or unsuccessful) in our relationship.

Differences make us unique, as we are all distinct individuals who come from different homes, backgrounds, and sometimes cultures. Often times, these differences appear attractive and seductive. Nonetheless, over time they become the source of conflict. Each of us learns to relate to others within the context of our family or environment, and many times what we have learned in the past is what we grow to expect.

No one person knows everything there is to know about having a relationship or dealing with conflict, but as a professional I can offer tangible, helpful advice—as well as teach you proven techniques and skills that have helped my clients improve or repair their relationships. The information in this book is a combination of theories and techniques that I have learned through school, continuing education, the practice of these theories with my clients, scientific studies, and the results that I have seen in my work with clients—as well as the application in my personal life. I will discuss why we repeatedly get stuck in the same problems, the nature of change, forgiveness, communication, expectations, love, friendship, trust, and the roadblocks that you could face as you work on your relationship, and much more. This book could help you by increasing your understanding about your difficulties, and teaching you new ways to relate to the one you love.

Before going any further, I want to point out that if you're in an abusive relationship either physically or emotionally, then this book is not for you. The theories and techniques in this book could lead you to be in vulnerable situations that may put you at risk. If you're in an abusive relationship, please, please consider talking to someone about your situation. There is help available, you can start by calling the National Domestic Violence Hotline at 1 (800) 799-7233, or going to their website at www.thehotline.org. Keep in mind that your phone and internet use can be monitored by your partner. It can be a difficult and lengthy process to leave an abusive relationship, but it's never too late.

The stories and dialogues of this book are inspired from real people, their names, genders, and circumstances have been changed to protect their identity, but the core issues remain true. If you know someone whose circumstances are similar to what I describe, it's merely a coincidence. Keep in mind that the issues I'll discuss in the remaining of this book are fairly common. I hope that you enjoy, learn, and reflect on the content of this book, but more so that you can use some of these concepts and suggestions, and apply them in your life. If you and your partner are willing, you can reinvent your relationship.

Chapter 1
LOVE & ATTACHMENT

I start this book with the concepts of love and attachment since this is usually where relationships start. Without love, many of the difficulties and challenges we face in life as a couple would quickly erode the relationship. More so, I often encounter confusions about love when working with individuals in long-term relationships. My clients tell me things like: "I'm not in-love with him/her anymore," "I don't know if I love my partner the same way," "I don't have the same passion about my partner." You may think some of the same things, because we have an idea of love that is highly influenced by mainstream culture: advertising, movies, TV shows, poems, songs, etc. Unfortunately, these influences create an unrealistic expectation about feelings, desires, and needs in relationships.

If you are in a long term relationship and have noticed that the love you feel for your partner is different from when you first got together, you're experiencing something absolutely normal that comes with the changes you encounter as a relationship ages and evolves. Anthropologists and researchers have identified three stages of love in humans (Fisher 1998; 2005): Lust, attraction, and attachment. It's believed that love evolves for mating and reproductive purposes, which allows us to live in long term relationships as we get older. Think about this: as our bodies age, even with the help of erectile dysfunction drugs, estrogen supplements, testosterone therapy, and hip replacements sex is not eternal. Let's examine these stages and their characteristics more closely.

Lust is mainly characterized by the craving for sexual gratification. Think about when you first started dating your partner, and even a kiss could fire up intense sexual feelings and desires. You probably experienced these same feelings with other individuals you dated in the past, even if you did not enter into long-term relationships with them. Individuals experience this desire for sexual gratification without specific selection of a partner, anyone could do. Many times, the drive to seek this sexual gratification is responsible for affairs, confusions about love, commitment, and more importantly unhappiness and self-doubt.

This stage of love is temporary, and it often doesn't last long. It may come and go in your relationship, but it's unfair to you and your partner to expect this stage to be permanent in your relationship. I have seen much doubt and questioning from individuals who seek to maintain this stage. They usually end up moving from one relationship to the next hoping that they can maintain this feeling, inevitably ending the relationship once lust ends—which could range from 6 months to 3 years depending on the individual.

Attraction is characterized by increased energy and focused attention on one or more potential mates, accompanied by feelings of exhilaration, intrusive thinking (obsession-like) about a mate, and the craving for emotional union with this mate or potential mate. When you're madly in love with someone, the person becomes the center of your world, and they take a special meaning in your life.

The attraction stage helps you be more selective than the earlier lust, since it can be influenced by childhood experiences, cultural forces, and individual choice. This attraction leads you to visualize yourself with your partner in the future, and you may ask yourself "Do we have the same values or goals in life?" or "Are we a good match for a life together?" This stage helps you decide if this person will be a good father or mother for future children, —or life partner if children are not in your future.

Attachment is characterized by the maintenance of close social contact, accompanied by feelings of calm, security, comfort, and emotional union with a mate. Love evolves from lust to attraction, and later to attachment in order to help you focus and concentrate your attention in one partner and tolerate him or her at least long enough to get through child rearing years. This attachment is what most people desire when they think of a long-term relationship. Feeling safe and secure is the motivation.

Love is a complex experience of excitement when things go well, but also of sadness and hurt when things fall apart. Therefore, love can bring great joy or great sorrow to your life. If you're experiencing a hard time in your relationship, you could identify with the pain that relationships can cause. However, your desire and motivation to work on this relationship is probably based on the happiness and joy you once experienced. Some researchers believe that love is not an emotion (Fisher 2006), but a powerful brain system that drives and motivates people to act. Think of what love has motivated you to do in the past and maybe the present. Whether in times of joy or sorrow, it's clear that love can have a great impact on your motivations and influence your actions. More so, studies show that falling in love affects intellectual areas of the brain and triggers the same sensation of euphoria experienced by people when they take cocaine (Ortigue, Bianchi-Demicheli, Patel, Frum, & Lewis 2010). You may be thinking that his helps to explain a few particularly poor choices from the past.

IS LOVE ENOUGH?

Unfortunately, love is not enough to maintain a relationship. Love can motivate actions or motivate you to work on a relationship, but to maintain a relationship takes two motivated individuals. Have you ever ended a relationship even though you loved that person? Have you been in a relationship with someone who said he or she loved you back, but his or her actions showed something different? Have you been repeatedly hurt by the person who says they love you? Have you ever loved someone who didn't feel the same way about you? These are all instances where love was not enough.

Commitment—defined as a long-term orientation toward a relationship, including intent to persist and feelings of psychological attachment (Wieselquist et al. 1999)—is a major factor in creating enduring long-term relationships. Without commitment, it's easier to move on to find the next "better" partner for you. In fact, scientific studies confirm that human beings are neurologically able to love more than one person at a time (Fisher 2005). Therefore, a strong sense of commitment is needed in long-term relationships. This helps to avoid distractions and urges to act from feelings of lust and attraction towards others than your long-term relationship partner.

Other factors that have been identified in order to secure long-term relationships are cooperation, trust, and loyalty (Beck 1989), and we'll examine each of these and more in detail throughout this book.

PATTERNS OF ATTACHMENT

In my work with couples, I have learned that in relationships the same problems come up over and over again, and many remain stuck in the same problem. These problems can develop in very different situations, which may seem unrelated for the untrained eye, but are rooted by the need to feel love in the form of attachment to a close person in our lives. Anything can start an argument: a look, an innocent action or lack of action, other people's comments or influence, how a situation is handled, and much more. Consciously or unconsciously, when we point out that our partner is doing or not doing something, we're looking for a response—something to let us know that he or she cares, that they love us, that we're a priority in their life—but often times the response can be disappointing. We all want to be special to another person, to feel important, to be desired, and ultimately to be loved and secure. These needs can lead us to do or say many irrational things such as chase, fight, insult and even bully a partner, which ultimately damages the relationship and decreases the chances of feeling loved and secure. People can easily engage in behaviors that work against their true objectives without even realizing it.

Learning to identify what behaviors are working against our objectives can be difficult because many times we engage in them unconsciously. We learn patterns of interaction through our relationship with caregivers since infancy (Bowlby 1958), which impact our future relationships without even realizing it. There is now an increasing amount of research evidence that suggests adult romantic relationships function in a way similar to infant-caregiver relationships, with some noteworthy exceptions of what may be considered acceptable behaviors for adults (Fraley, 2010). The following is the classification of attachment patterns for adult interactions with loving partners: Secure Attachment, Anxious-Preoccupied Attachment, Dismissive-Avoidant Attachment, and Fearful-Avoidant Attachment (Hazan and Shaver 1987; 1990; 1994). Let's take a look at these in more detail:

Secure Attachment individuals can balance intimacy and independence, and they usually have a positive view of themselves, their partners and their relationships. Unsurprisingly, secure attachment individuals can have healthier and happier relationships with little effort. These individuals usually have high self-esteem and can trust their partner unless the trust is broken.

Anxious-Preoccupied individuals have a hard time trusting. They desperately want to feel intimacy, and may exhibit intense emotional expressiveness, worrying, and impulsive behaviors in their relationships. They often seek an increased approval from partners, usually leading to a sense of dependency or "neediness". They have less positive views about themselves and their partners. These individuals are easily stressed in their relationships and may exhibit aggressive behaviors in order to seek responses from partners. They over-analyze their partner's actions and statements, which leads to assuming their partners' intentions are untrustworthy. Later they may react impulsively based on their assumptions. I usually see anxious-preoccupied clients in couples due to non-grounded jealousy or insecurities about their relationship.

In my work with anxious-preoccupied individuals I first try to help them identify how their actions affect their partners, since often they have not realized how they can be influencing their feelings of insecurity. I work with them on challenging the irrational thoughts that lead to the distrust (you can learn more about challenging irrational thoughts in Chapter 7), since many times their patterns of thinking are creating feelings which may not be based in any real evidence. If there is any factual evidence that could be worrisome about a partner's commitment to the relationship, I would urge them to specifically identify their partner's behaviors that lead to the perceived mistrust. I also stress fostering more effective communication to let their partners know how their actions are triggering their insecurities and possibly recruit the partner's help. It's common that after years of being accused of being distrustful, partners start to purposely hide information or lie in order to avoid emotional or explosive confrontations. The hiding and lying can create more reasons to be distrustful, thereby creating an ongoing negative cycle of interaction that feeds itself. We'll look at common negative cycles of interaction in the next chapter.

Dismissive-Avoidant individuals aspire to a high level of independence, and may even appear to avoid attachment or closeness altogether. These individuals perceive themselves as self-sufficient and not needing close relationships. They suppress their feelings, and deal with rejection by distancing themselves from partners of whom they usually have a poor opinion. Dismissive-avoidant individuals tend to avoid arguments since "it's a waste of time," communicating contempt towards their partner. Dismissive-avoidant individuals usually come into therapy because their partner forces them, since they would prefer to avoid talking about their feelings or addressing any conflicts in their relationships.

With dismissive-avoidant individuals, developing empathy is crucial. By putting themselves in their partner's shoes they could become more empathetic towards their partner. Many times, accessing a situation from a different perspective can do a lot for the understanding of a problem. Simply recognizing the importance of a partner and the role they play in their life can help the dismissive-avoidant individual challenge the belief that they do not need a close relationship. Exploring feelings that come along with having a close relationship can also help them gain insight into how great it can feel to have someone special in our lives.

Fearful-avoidant individuals go back and forward about their feelings towards close relationships, both desiring closeness and feeling uncomfortable with it. They often have difficulty trusting their partners and see themselves as unworthy. They may avoid intimacy and suppress their feelings. Typically these individuals rarely trust their partners, and their insecurities stem from low self-worth and low self esteem. They rarely take risks or try new approaches towards their partners. Many will avoid confronting problems for fear of losing their partners. As well, if they take the risk to trust and are let down, this can become an impactful event, which will only reinforce their existing fears.

When working with fearful-avoidant individuals I try to help them identify the fear hiding behind their avoidance, since they're usually not aware of it. Most people do not like to admit that they are afraid, therefore fear can be called many different names such as stress, preoccupation, worry, dread, anxiety, discomfort, and much more. Talking about fears can be a challenge for many, especially if they are working hard to suppress it. Part of the work towards meaningful change can be to help someone feel comfortable expressing their fears about closeness, in an effort to communicate it to their partners.

After learning about the different relational patterns, you can see how if we combine these traits it can be pretty difficult for people to relate to one another. Imagine how a couple made up from a dismissive-avoidant individual and a fearful-avoidant individual, could solve any difficulties. If they're both trying to avoid each other and suppress their feelings, how can anything be addressed in a meaningful way? Here is an example of what their interactions can be like:

Patty (fearful-avoidant): You have been working a lot lately. We don't spend time together anymore.

Henry (dismissive-avoidant): I'm tired. I'm too stressed out about work. I don't have it in me.

Patty: Never mind, I can have fun alone. I shouldn't wait for you. I don't need you.

Henry: Are you going to start again? Why can't you just let me be? I'm not as needy as you are.

Patty: No worries, I won't ask you again.

Henry: That's what you always say, but you can't stick to it can you?

Patty: I don't even know why I keep trying, you just don't care.

Of course, we all share small traits of all of the previous classifications, but more often than not we may find our behavior gradually falling under one of them. Remember, these relating behaviors are usually learned at an early age and are mostly unconscious—we aren't doing them on purpose. Our brain is programmed to work this way when interacting with other important people in our lives, since these may apply not only to our partner, but also to close friends, family members, children, and more. The first step to change is to identify that this is happening. Once you accept that it's a problem in your life you can take steps to make things different. Change is not an easy process, but it is possible. With determination and commitment you can learn new ways to relate to others close to you. Because change is a difficult process, many seek therapeutic help, but it may not be necessary. Learning more effective ways to communicate your emotions can be useful if you're trying to alter a negative pattern of interaction. We'll focus on communication techniques in Chapter 4, so you can learn and apply new techniques and see what kind of results you can get.

By implementing the suggestions and techniques that I will cover in the following chapters, I am confident you can achieve positive results in your own relationship. However, if these are too difficult you can consider talking to a professional to help you and guide you through your efforts to make changes in your life.

EXERCISE

The following are questions to help you identify the effect that your relating behavioral patterns have on your relationship. Being honest with yourself is important, so think through and answer the following questions as truthfully as possible:

1. Do you become overly emotional when seeking answers from your partner? If yes, what is your partner's reaction?
2. Do you have a hard time trusting your partner? If yes, do you have factual evidence of this?
3. Do you shut down and avoid your partner? If yes, what do you think your partner feels when you avoid her/him?
4. What do you think your partner wants/expect from you?
5. Are you avoiding your partner because you're worried about his/her reactions?
6. What would happen if your partner knew how you *really* felt about your relationship?
7. What pattern of interaction best fit your relational pattern?
8. What is your objective when you approach/avoid your partner?
9. Did you get the results you expect?

Answering these questions can help you gain some insight into how your actions can be working against your objective to feel safe, secure, and connected in your relationship.

Chapter 2

BEING STUCK & MOVING TOWARD CHANGE

"When we are no longer able to change a situation —
we are challenged to change ourselves."
—Viktor E. Frankl

How do we go from being happily in love to being stuck in a miserable relationship? First, the period of lust and attraction ends, and we end up with individuals who have different attachment needs than ours. Many times, at this point in the relationships major investments in life have been made with a partner, and there are common interests such as children, property, and more. Routine also sets in, and it starts to look like much of the same. If conflict becomes the routine, and tension floats around, it's more likely the couple is questioning their involvement, saying mean things to each other (or thinking them) or starting to wonder if it's worth the effort. Many may consider ending the relationship or divorcing after a while. They might think: "This relationship makes me unhappy, so ending the relationship may help me feel happier." However, ending the relationship may not necessarily be the answer, and working on improving it instead may actually be worth it. Interestingly, a national survey concluded that people who were unhappy in their relationships did not feel happier after divorce (Waite et al. 2002).

Being stuck in a relationship that makes you suffer is not easy, but identifying the things that may be contributing to the conflict could help you by allowing you to do something about it, if possible. In the previous chapter I mentioned how we learn to relate to others early in life, which leads to a series of patterns of behaviors. Over time, couples also develop pretty consistent patterns of interaction during conflictive situations. When you have two individuals in a relationship, and each one has a specific pattern of interaction and different attachment needs, the combination of the two can be either strengthening or destructive to the relationship. The latter is called a negative cycle of interaction (Greenberg & Johnson 1998; 2010), and this cycle is the same in every conflict or difficulty, despite what originates the situation. It's important to identify these negative cycles of interactions between couples, which lead them to be "stuck" and unable to move towards positive interactions. Just like individual attachment patterns have been identified and classified, couples patterns have also been identified and classified: Constructive Engagement, Mutual Avoidance, Destructive Engagement, and Engage-Distance (Fruzzetti 2006).

CONSTRUCTIVE ENGAGEMENT

This happens when couples can bring up issues or disagreement when it's relevant in a constructive, non-aggressive and clear manner. This cycle is the ideal way of relating, since it promotes respect, validation, understanding, and compromise. Couples who engage in this positive cycle of interaction are able to move on from their disagreements, even if they cannot find a permanent solution to the problem. Being able to express their feelings and explore the conflict can help the couple gain understanding for each other, and eventually bring the couple closer.

Ex. Frank, Diana and their son come back from Diana's parents' residence. Frank seems frustrated and tells Diana about his feelings.

Frank: I don't like it when your mom tells me how I should clean up after Tommy after he eats. She criticizes everything I do towards Tommy and you just stand there, it makes me think that you agree with her. I feel like you two are against me. *Here Frank expresses his feelings in a non-aggressive clear manner.*

Diana: Honey, I'm sorry that you feel this way. I haven't noticed that she does it; I guess I haven't reacted because I haven't noticed. But I can see how you would not like it. *Diana validates Frank's feelings.*

Frank: She does it every time she gets a chance and it's getting really old.

Diana: You sound frustrated. I wouldn't like it if someone told me how to act towards Tommy either (*Diana express understanding once again*). Is there something that I can do to make the situation better (*Diana also offers help and an opportunity to compromise*)?

Frank: Not really. Well, maybe you could say something to her next time it happens.

Diana: I may need you to signal me that it is happening so I can say something.

Frank: I will.

Diana: How about if I say, "Mom, we do things differently and it works for us."

Frank: I would like that. Maybe you can add, "Frank knows what he is doing!"

Diana: I can totally do that.

Frank: I guess that would help me feel like you are supportive towards me.

Diana: Of course I am, and I want to make sure I show you that I am.

Frank: Thanks. Do you want to watch *House of Cards* while Tommy takes a nap?

Diana: Sure. I love Kevin Spacey in that role.

Frank: Me too, babe. *Lastly, the conversation moves to a constructive solution finding outcome.*

After reading this example you may be thinking "this is too good to be true," but it's possible if you can learn to avoid aggressive reactions (more on that in Chapter 7) and tune in to what your partner is asking from you—in this case "support." If you can meet or at least attempt to meet your partner's need or request, you'll be contributing to a stronger and more intimate relationship.

MUTUAL AVOIDANCE

This pattern of negative interaction takes place when both partners deal with conflict and difficulty by avoiding it. Usually, in the beginning of the relationship one partner brings up a disagreement and is faced with highly emotional reactions from their partner, which as a result creates reciprocal highly emotional reactions from the partner who wanted to address the issue. After this interaction takes place for some time, partners choose to avoid bringing up difficult subjects in order to prevent negative emotional interactions. As a result, their differences are not being solved and they grow distant from each other, even though they may not argue often.

Ex. Frank and Diana return back from Diana's parents' residence. Frank seems frustrated, but he doesn't tell her about his feelings.

Frank: (Quiet during the ride home, and once at home goes straight to watch TV.)

Diana: (Realizes that Frank is upset about something and probably thinks: "Here he goes again, I can't take his moods. I better stay away from him.")

DESTRUCTIVE ENGAGEMENT

This happens when both partners become easily aggressive and defensive during interactions, which leads to ineffective and inappropriate language and behaviors that are often regretted later on. Both individuals become vulnerable to each other's comments or statements and are quick to react. An interaction does not necessarily have to start out negatively, but it tends to end that way. These couples often struggle with impulsive, aggressive behaviors towards one another due to emotional outbursts.

Ex. Frank and Diana came back from Diana's parents' residence. Frank seems frustrated and tells Diana about his feelings.

Frank: I don't like it when your mom tells me how I should clean up Tommy after he eats. She criticizes everything I do towards Tommy and you just f****g stand there, it makes me think that you agree with her. I feel like you two are against me.

Diana: What are you talking about? My mom didn't do anything. You're crazy.

Frank: You're always defending your family. What about me? You just use me for my money so you don't have to work!

Diana: You're being an idiot.

Frank: I don't even know why I married you. I should have known then that you're selfish and didn't really love me.

Diana: I don't know why I married you either, I should have listened to my mom.

Frank: That's exactly what I'm talking about. It's like that time you believed your mom over me. Yes, you should have listened to your mom. It would have made my life easier.

Two hours later

Frank: (Shuts down door and goes to sleep in the living room).

Diana: (Throws pillows at him before she goes to bed).

This pattern can easily end up in violence, due to the high aggressiveness and impulsivity on both sides.

ENGAGE-DISTANCE

This pattern of interaction is characterized by partners having different ways to deal with conflict. One partner easily becomes aggressive, defensive, and struggles with impulsive behaviors. The other partner distances his or herself by avoiding addressing of any difficult subjects in order to prevent negative emotional interactions ("shutting down"). This is a common cycle between couples, but difficult since partners move in opposite directions from each other. In this pattern, arguments are not usually solved.

Ex. Frank and Diana return from Diana's parents' residence. Frank seems frustrated and tells Diana about his feelings.

Frank: I don't like it when your mom tells me how I should clean up Tommy after he eats. She criticizes everything I do towards Tommy and you just stand there, it makes me think that you agree with her. I feel like you two are against me.

Diana: Are you going to start again?

Frank: What do you mean? I'm only trying to tell you how I feel. Why can't you stand up for me?

Diana: I don't know what to tell you.

Frank: You never have anything to say. It's like talking to a wall, I don't get any responses. Do you even have any feelings? Do you care about me?

Diana: (Rolls her eyes) Look, I have to go get milk for tomorrow.

Frank: Of course. Run away like you always do.

In order to become unstuck from these negative cycles one or both partners would have to change the approach to the interaction. Attempts to change an approach would be a lot easier if couples were better able to regulate their emotions in an effort to have more effective and constructive discussions. I will discuss emotion regulation later on in Chapter 7. Remember, all couples—including the ones that fit into the Constructive Engagement cycle—have arguments. It's how they deal with their differences and disagreements that can make a difference in their interactions and ultimately the relationship. What pattern do you think fits your relationship interactions?

IT'S NOT ABOUT BEING "RIGHT"

I have noticed that at times being stuck in these cycles can be influenced by a need to "win" or be "right" in regards to an argument or the way to do something "the right way". Therefore, the objective of the interaction is to "win" or prove your partner to be wrong at any cost. Often times, competitive or alpha personalities tend to follow an urge to succeed. It's important that you realize that so-called winning can get in the way of the relationship you want to have. Sometimes, today's loss can turn into tomorrow's win. Being in a relationship is not about winning or losing, and you can't always be right, believe it or not. Winning or being "right" is about perception.

If you want a pair of shoes and are used to paying $100 for them, finding a sale for $80 shoes is a win. On the other hand, if you're used to paying $40 for shoes, that same sale doesn't look so great. In another example, one person may think that the right way to fold a t-shirt is to part it with three folds, while the other person "knows" that everyone folds t-shirts into two folds. So, I usually explain to my clients that they're both right, and that they're both wrong. There is not ONE way to do things, there are many. Maybe you can learn something from your partner, or the other way around.

WHY CHANGE?

Research suggests that relationship quality is one of the most sound predictors of the perceived need for relationship adjustment (Hassebrauk & Fehr, 2002). Therefore, if you're unhappy with your relationship you'll most likely seek change, either by your own efforts and or your partner's. By looking at multiple studies across different cultures and age groups, Hassebrauk and Fehr identified four common themes that are of central importance to relationship quality: intimacy, agreement, independence, and sexuality. The conclusion of these studies has been confirmed and demonstrated in my work with couples, when partners come into therapy seeking help to address deficits in the quality of their relationship.

Studies have also recognized that individuals are profit-oriented concerning exchanges in their relationships, to the extent that those who perceive they are involved in an unbalanced relationship manifest distress (Sprecher, 2001). The greater the distress caused by an unbalanced relationship, the greater the effort they will attempt to place towards eliminating the distress and restoring fairness. As they face the distress in their relationship, they start experiencing a process of change.

Change is described as a process involving progress through a series of stages (Prochaska & Velicer, 1997). The stages of change identified by Prochaska and Diclemente, (1983) known as the Transtheoretical Model of Change, (TTM) are : 1. Precontemplation, 2. Contemplation, 3. Preparation, 4. Action, 5. Maintenance, 6. Relapse.

Even though change has been mostly defined in terms of individuals and little research has been done with the stages of change in relation to couples' processes of change, I believe the TTM to be relevant to the understanding of each partner's process in the quest to modify behaviors in a loving a relationship. Of the few studies done, it was determined that changing a relationship of two is not an individual process (LaCoursiere, 2008). Let's look at this model more closely applied towards individuals in a loving relationship and the process of positively modifying their relationship.

The Precontemplation Stage (not ready) describes an individual who is either unaware of their actions and the effects they have on self and/or others, or is not thinking about changing. At times, others around may be aware and have even brought it up to their attention. However, the individual may not be aware of how their actions influence the negative cycle of interaction (from Chapter 2) in their relationship's distress. This stage is also referred to as being "in denial." For some, it may be easier to blame others for their problems, but it can be difficult to accept that something they're doing can contribute to their own problems in a relationship. Everyone is not ready or willing to take responsibility for the negative consequences caused by their actions, nor can you force them.

The Contemplation Stage (getting ready) describes an individual who is thinking about changing, but is not yet committed to take action. Many times the cost of changing can seem too much. A factor resembling contemplation is called ambivalence (Miller & Tonigan 1996). At this stage an individual goes back and forward about the need to change; he or she may not be sure that it can be done. Sometimes they may think about behaving towards their partner in a different manner, but aren't ready to follow through. The possible consequences gained do not seem worth the effort, or they may wait for "the right time" to do it. An individual may spend time weighing the pros and cons of changing. E.g. "It's going to take too much work," "I'll wait until things get better/worse," or "It must not be that bad since we haven't talked about separation." Someone in this stage may or may not share thoughts of ambivalence with their partner.

The Preparation Stage (ready) describes someone intending to make changes in the immediate future. At this point the individual balancing or weighing pros and cons has decided that making changes in their relationship is worth the price and consequences. He or she comes up with an objective and may make plans about the change (how and when it's going to happen). This may look like: buying and reading a self-help book (like the one you're reading), researching articles on the internet, looking for a therapist, calling to find out prices, and even making an appointment. This stage refers to getting ready for action. Those in this stage may or may not share the plan with the partner.

The Action Stage describes those who have made specific modifications in their thinking and behaviors, which previously led to conflict, or distress in their relationship. This is probably due to gaining understanding of thought and behavior patterns that influenced conflict and negative interactions between self and partner, as well as the substitution of more constructive thought and behavior patterns. Acting on new advice of others, articles, books, a professional, or even self-realization can take trial and error.

The Maintenance Stage describes those who have achieved a positive change in their relationship and are enjoying the gains obtained as a result of it. At this stage, they work on preventing relapsing to earlier stages, and the modifications in thinking and behavior take less effort. People may be less tempted to relapse if they are feeling more confident in their ability to make changes and stick to them. Successful change usually involves passing through each stage in the proper sequence, since skipping stages is likely to result in relapse (Prochaska, DiClemente, & Norcross, 1992).

Relapse describes individuals reverting from any stage to an earlier stage of change. Relapse is one form of regression, involving regression from action or maintenance to an earlier stage. It's possible to regress from any stage to an earlier stage, but research demonstrates that few individuals regress all the way to the precontemplation stage; the vast majority regress to contemplating or preparation (Prochaska & DiClemente, 1983).

My experience working with couples is that both partners are not usually in the same stage of change. It's often the case that one partner is more motivated to make changes than the other. However, through therapy, both partners can end up making positive modifications towards the improvement of the relationship. Even if one individual makes changes, this will inevitably affect the dynamic of the relationship (O'Leary, 1999). It's also useful to keep in mind that even if more gains are acquired from the changing aspects of the relationship, it is likely that the couple still continues to experience distress. The change will require an adjustment period for the couple as a whole. This distress I'm referring to is most likely to come from the last five stages, which is where the change is likely to be observed. The later stages of the process are where the couple is now *doing* instead of *experiencing*. More so, where the couple is re-engineering behaviors, and all the while trying to support one another in their endeavors (LaCoursiere, 2008).

Identifying the above stages may be useful to you and your partner, but it's also important to consider what may prevent people from making changes in relationships, since the complexity of two individuals can clearly add some limitations to one person's efforts to change. You can learn more about factors that prevent change or progress in Chapter 13 on this book.

Are you ready to make changes? The term *readiness* typically implies the use of motivation as well as self-efficacy when looking at an individual's intent to change a specific behavior. Studies show that readiness to change refers to affect (feelings or emotions) and cognitions (knowledge or perception) that lead to efforts to change (Bradford, 2012). I want you to consider that readiness to change one behavior is completely independent of readiness to change a separate behavior (Schneider, 2003); therefore, you or your partner can experience different stages in regard to different behaviors that may have been identified as necessary to change. For example, if your partner wants you to start working out and eating healthier in an effort to have a healthier lifestyle, you may contemplate and even prepare to work out, but still be stuck on the precontemplation stage in regards to eating healthier. Another consideration is that what is a positive change for you, may be problematic for your partner. For instance, asking your partner to rinse the dishes before placing them in the dishwasher may seem like common sense to you, yet be considered a waste of precious water for your partner.

Throughout this book I will provide you with specific guidance in the form of tools, techniques, tips or suggestions to help you and your partner make these necessary changes in an effort to improve your relationship.

Chapter 3
FORGIVENESS

The weak can never forgive. Forgiveness is the attribute of the strong."
—Mahatma Gandhi

Forgiveness is a key aspect of being in a relationship; as imperfect human beings, we hurt or offend others unintentionally, which is why forgiveness is needed to give our partner another chance to do better the next time—or give ourselves another chance. Without forgiveness it would be very difficult to be in a relationship because life as a couple would turn into a never-ending war. Furthermore, scientific studies have documented the association between forgiveness and marital satisfaction (Fincham, Beach, Davilla, 2004), since it communicates conflict resolution between partners. Forgiveness has been defined as the action of giving up resentment, indignation or anger caused by an offense committed by another or ourselves ("Forgiveness", 2014). It's a voluntary change of destructive behaviors directed against the damage that has been done for other, more constructive behaviors. Forgiveness is not a single act that is done in a given time, but an ongoing process that doesn't happen overnight.

Depending on a situation, its frequency, and the individual, forgiveness can be a very difficult process. Some offences may seem impossible to forgive for some, but easier for others. Think about an extreme situation such as abuse (physical or emotional) compared to someone being late to your meeting or date. Forgiveness is also about perception, what one can tolerate and what another cannot tolerate is not the same. If your partner forgets to take out the trash once or twice, it may be easy to forgive him or her or give and them the benefit of the doubt. However, if your partner forgets to take out the trash more often than not, it may get difficult to let go. In the same nature, if a partner uses derogatory names during an argument once it may be easier to forgive than if this happens regularly.

What tends to make it more difficult to forgive our partner is that we make our own assumptions or conclusions about "**why**" something is happening or not happening. Think back to the previous example where you ask your partner to take out the trash; if they forget once or twice you can easily conclude they forgot or have been busy lately. On the other hand, if you ask your partner to take out the trash and they neglect to do it most of the times you ask, you may start assuming or concluding that he/she doesn't care about your requests, your feelings, your efforts, or that they are doing it on purpose to upset you. In this example, our minds make sense of what is happening or not happening by attributing "good reasons" to what we don't know for sure. By contrasting these two, it can be said that it would be a lot easier to forgive someone who is busy or forgets to take out the trash once or twice, but it may be more difficult to forgive someone who always forgets to take out the trash "because he/she doesn't care."

Forgiveness is promoted as a virtue in many different religious beliefs: Christianity, Judaism, Islam, Buddhism, Hinduism, and many others. Religions usually emphasize forgiveness as a major component of their teachings. This religious aspect can make forgiveness a sought-after objective, but I have seen people who struggle with forgiveness when they perceive it is expected from them by their religious communities. As I mentioned before, forgiveness is a process that takes time, so it's an individual process that can take different amounts of time for different wrongdoings, while also factoring in the individual's ability and willingness to forgive. There is not a set standard time frame that it would take to complete the process, and if rushed it can become even more complicated.

When you hurt, your immediate reaction is to go against logic and towards those who hurt you. This reaction is natural due to our fight or flight instinct (see Chapter 7), but it has its problems. Going against the one who hurt you can seem like it would be rewarding, but it usually isn't—because now you can be the cause of pain toward another, and as a result additional feelings can develop such as guilt or shame, further complicating the situation. Therefore you have the original resentment, indignation, and anger plus the guilt or shame that can come after revenge. All of this results in a complex mixture of feelings, which can lead to suffering. If you're attacking the person who hurt you, forgiveness will not be possible. One way to overcome the fear and anger is to recall the hurt and accept the pain for what it is, as we will discuss next.

The following are five steps to be completed in an effort to facilitate the process of forgiveness. These steps can be invaluable in achieving the fullest extent of forgiveness. The **Five Steps to Forgiveness** are:

1. Recall the hurt, 2. Empathize with the one who hurt you, 3. Offer the Altruistic gift of forgiveness, 4. Make a commitment to forgive, 5. Hold on to the forgiveness (Worthinton 2005).

RECALL THE HURT

This can be a difficult step, since naturally we try to escape hurt mentally and physically (we can do this by masking it with substance abuse or addictions such as alcohol or drugs, or engaging in self-destructive behaviors like self injury, sex addiction, or suicide attempts). Escaping thoughts is more difficult and can be highly frustrating since you may not have the skills to stop them. In order to overcome the fear and anger that has been caused, recalling the feelings of hurt and working towards accepting the pain for what it is can help you start the process of forgiveness. Again, this can be a difficult task to do on your own. Seeking help can facilitate the process, since accepting a hurtful and painful event can be difficult for anyone. Recalling the hurt can be done by talking to a close friend or a family member who can listen in a safe environment, or talking to a professional. Writing about the hurtful event and/or feelings can also be a way of recalling the hurt.

EMPATHIZE WITH THE ONE WHO HURT YOU

This step is about trying to understand the other person—not from your own perspective, but from that of the other person. The purpose is not to find an excuse for them, but to find an explanation that you can live with, and that can help you let go of the fear and anger. This can be extremely difficult for many, depending on the wrongdoing that took place. You may never understand the reason why someone would do such a thing, especially if you could not imagine doing anything remotely similar to the person you love. It's easier to have empathy for someone who is not hurting you anymore. One way to empathize with the one who hurt you is by thinking about their painful experiences, shortcomings, limitations, and fears.

OFFER THE ALTRUISTIC GIFT OF FORGIVENESS

Think of a time when you felt guilty about hurting another and how that person forgave you. Try to remember how grateful you felt. We all have caused pain or hurt to others, especially the ones we care most about such as our partners, our parents and our children. By allowing yourself to think about a time when someone forgave you, you can experience empathy for the one who hurt you that may seek your forgiveness.

MAKE A COMMITMENT TO FORGIVE

This commitment is better done publicly so you don't have a chance to back up later. At times, you may want to forgive your partner, but you hold back or do not communicate your forgiveness. This can create space between you and your partner when you could be enjoying each other's love and affection. To help you recommit to forgive, thinking about the positive qualities your partner has and the future memories you could build together can help.

HOLD ON TO THE FORGIVENESS

From time to time, memories of the hurtful event will resurface even after you have forgiven your partner. These memories are usually less intense than they were before you forgave him/her. You may have to remind yourself that you chose to forgive. Think about the great memories you have built since you chose to forgive them; this can help reassure you of your previous decision to forgive. Think about the strengths your partner has and the way they can make you feel loved. Think about their actions of remorse towards you.

I would like to clarify that forgiveness does not necessarily include reconciliation. To forgive or ask for forgiveness are personal choices that do not require the assistance of another person. However, reconciliation is for two. In order to achieve reconciliation both partners have to consciously work towards it, one partner by working the process of forgiveness and the other by behaving in a way to promote trust, (see Chapter 11). Forgiveness does not have to restore the relationship with someone who most likely can return to harm you. If your partner cannot bring themselves to stop lying, end an affair, or if you have not left an abusive relationship, then it will be close to impossible to start the process of forgiveness—mostly because the feelings of hurt are continuously present. Forgiveness can be extremely difficult if not impossible while you're still being hurt. One way to help facilitate the process of forgiveness if your partner cannot stop themselves is by making the decision to stop the situation yourself. This may mean leaving or asking for space from the situation that is causing the hurt or pain, either physically or emotionally.

FORGIVENESS IS NOT:

Forgiveness does not mean forgetting what happened; as I mentioned before, memories from the hurtful event will come back. You will not forget, but can choose to change destructive behaviors to positive behaviors towards your partner, such as recommitting to forgive and holding on to the forgiveness. Remember, forgiveness is not justifying the offense or minimizing it. However, you could benefit from empathizing with your partner about their actions that hurt you. Forgiveness is not necessarily to raise the penalty of the offender and not suffer the consequences of their actions. Reconciliation requires that your partner make a restitution of the damage he/she has done to you, if possible. Forgiveness is for the forgiver to stop searching actively for justice and is sparing with the consequences, since the expected justice will not necessarily bring emotional release. Finally, forgiveness is not a sign of weakness, because it is not giving permission to your partner to hurt you again, but instead being careful not to let them hurt you again by learning from the situation and setting limits. In my work I have encountered individuals who struggle with confusion about forgiveness and weakness, since they believe that holding on to the hurt can keep you "strong." The reality is just the opposite; as Mahatma Gandhi stated "The weak can never forgive. Forgiveness is the attribute of the strong."

I would like to share the story of Samantha, who came into therapy because she was unhappy with her relationship. A year prior to this, Samantha's husband got caught stealing from his job. He was penalized by the law and the loss of professional licenses which led to financial struggles, in addition to the shame associated with his actions. During the initial assessment in therapy, she was able to identify that her feelings about her relationship originated from the anger and resentment towards her husband since he had been caught. She was struggling to meet the expectations of her religious community to forgive her husband given his public signs of repentance; even Samantha admitted that he was actively apologizing and working towards making amends for his actions with his family. Samantha was growing frustrated with herself and would say things like "what is wrong with me?" She was struggling to accept her husband's actions and her own feelings, which prevented her from starting the process of forgiveness. Samantha expressed her difficulty empathizing with her husband, and she also explained that her husband had kept his feelings and insecurities hidden from her until the incident. A great deal of Samantha's hurt and disappointment was rooted in the fact that her husband had to wait to get caught and punished to share his feelings and insecurities with her. Despite Samantha's struggles with forgiving her husband, her commitment to him and her family was a priority which helped her stay motivated during difficult times throughout the process of forgiveness.

WHEN NOT TO FORGIVE

At times forgiving can be more damaging than moving on. In these cases, injuries are so deep or the betrayal was so grave and serious that forgiving will be psychologically damaging for the betrayed individual. Some wounds cannot be reconciled because the individual may never understand the motivation behind betrayal (Gottman 2011).

The following questions can help you in your efforts to forgive your partner for his/her wrongdoing:

1. What impact has the experience of hurt/pain had in your relationship?
2. What feelings do you have towards your partner after the hurt/pain that you suffered?
3. How did the hurt/pain make you feel about yourself?
4. What changes have occurred within you that make it possible for you to consider forgiving your partner?
5. What, if anything, has your partner said or done that has allowed you to consider forgiving him/her?
6. Why are you choosing to begin the process of forgiveness towards your partner?
7. How would you characterize your present relationship with your partner?
8. Is this the relationship you want to have with him/her?
9. What thoughts or feelings do you have about the future of your relationship?
10. What do you want your relationship to be like? Do you think that is possible to achieve it with your partner?
11. Review your responses to the questions and use them to help you consider your decision to forgive your partner if needed.

Hopefully after reading this chapter you can agree that forgiveness is an essential ability in order to have a long and stable relationship. In addition, studies have consistently shown that forgiveness reduces hostility, chronic anger, fear and stress, while increasing optimism and bringing health benefits (Lawler et al. 2005; Whorthington et al. 2007). If you have difficulty forgiving partner and others for their wrongdoings, try using the previous question and steps to help you throughout this difficult process. You could soon be on your way to feeling more positive emotions towards yourself and your loved ones.

Chapter 4
COMMUNICATION

Good words are worth much, and cost little.
—**George Herbert**

I f you reached this chapter thinking: "finally, this is my problem!" you're not alone; the majority of couples seeking professional help in their relationships report problems in this area. Moreover, research has shown over time that communication is one of the most reported problems areas of couples (Storaasli & Markman, 1990; Miller et al., 2003; Whisman, Dixon, & Johnson, 1997). Talking about problems or arguing is a normal part of relationships. We all have different opinions and views about the world around us, so it's only natural that we have differences. However, arguing can become so frequent and intense that it seems like the there is no hope for a relationship. We all have different approaches and opinions, based on what we have learned through our life experiences up to now. Most of us could agree that talking about problems with your partner (or anyone, really) can be uncomfortable and may potentially end up in arguments and fights without really solving the problem. If you are one of the lucky people in the world who was taught how to communicate properly early on, don't worry about reading this chapter. However, if your attempts to communicate are not as successful as you wish they were, this chapter can help.

You may have learned growing up that you don't talk about problems in an effort to avoid arguments; on the other hand you may have learned that talking about what is wrong can help you solve it. Either way, if your partner has an opposite approach, you may struggle with these moments and find yourself stuck in a negative cycle of interaction like we discussed earlier in Chapter 2.

If you struggle to express your feelings and you're hesitant to address an issue that bothers you with your partner, you may have grown up in a home where many things were left unsaid, perhaps to avoid punishment or upsetting others. Maybe your partner struggles to express himself/herself. Not discussing feelings was common in past generations, when parenting styles were more strict and rigid in regard to expressing anything that may bring out emotions. Information was less available, and children did not have as many choices as they have today. The problem with not expressing feelings or opinions about an issue that is important to you is that the feelings about the issue accumulate inside of you. When you have had enough (and we all have our limit), you will most likely explode. Exploding can look different for different people, but usually it's doing or saying something that you will later regret. In addition to bottling up your feelings, the problem continues since your partner may not be aware how important this is for you. Therefore, you may not be giving your partner a chance to please you or consider your feelings about the situation.

On the other hand, if you're the kind of person who was taught to talk about problems, you may not be specific enough in your communication for your partner to really understand why something bothers you or offends you. This can be frustrating, because you may feel like you tell your partner about your feelings all the time, but he/she does not care. More so, you may grow discouraged from continuing to express how you feel in order to avoid feeling disappointed by your partner. However, the reality is that you are probably disappointed regardless.

Information is valuable whether it is in the workplace or at home. If you are at work and are asked to complete a task, but have not been given all of the information about what is expected from you or the task, you may have to fill in some of the blanks, make some assumptions and hope your efforts are enough. Sometimes they may be, other times not so much. In the same light, if your partner asks you to do something but is not clear about what they want, you may put your best efforts forth, and it still may not be enough.

THREE TYPES OF COMMUNICATIONS

Let's take some time to go over the three types of communication in an effort to explore your own tendencies.

Non-Assertive is usually characterized by a lack of expression of one's wants, needs or desires. This individual mostly ignores their own rights and lets others infringe upon them. Often, he or she may not feel deserving of them. If they decide to express a need it tends to be done indirectly, and as a result they are easily hurt and disappointed in relationships. This in turn can lead to feelings of anxiety, and even anger later. This individual usually avoids conflict, unpleasant and risky situations, feels "used" and non-valued by others, and accumulates anger until it reaches their limit, and can eventually explode.

Assertive usually expresses and asserts their own rights in a way that the rights of others are taken into consideration. This individual tends to be honest, and directly expressive of feelings, needs and desires. He/she is self-motivated and most likely has a high self-esteem and confidence. The result of this type of communication is feeling valued by self and others. Their needs in relationships are mostly met, and relationships tend to be more honest and freer.

Being assertive can definitely be challenging, especially if it does not come naturally, but it's a skill that can be learned through constant practice and dedication. If you feel that you are not being assertive in your communication, it's important to start making an effort towards that goal so you can experience the results for yourself and your relationship. You can learn some tools to communicate assertively later in this chapter.

Aggressive communication usually leads to many conflicts in everyday life, since it's expressing one's own rights at the expense of others. Many times these people are perceived as accusatory or manipulative. They tend to have inappropriate outbursts of hostile overreaction towards situations, and may even want to humiliate or get even with others, whom they tend to put down. This person may be "brutally honest" at the expense of other's feelings. Most individuals who engage in aggressive communication feel angry, resentful, and at times superior to others, but possibly guilty for their actions later on.

The following are examples of what these communicators sound like:

Non-Assertive: It really doesn't matter. Don't worry (when it does matter).

Assertive: I don't think that you understand what I mean. Let's try again.

Aggressive: You're not listening to me, you never do. Stop being so selfish.

Remember that these types of communications are usually learned through our role models or through our unique life experiences. Being non-assertive or aggressive will only lead to frustration, disappointment about oneself and others, and internal and external conflicts in relationships. If you have identified that you communicate either in a non-assertive or aggressive manner, continue reading the following suggestions, since they could help you communicate your needs, feelings, and desires in a more assertive and effective manner. Talking about differences can actually be very productive for a couple, but what tends to get on the way is that they may not know how to talk about differences and/or emotions may get in the way of your communication. I will discuss emotion regulation later on in Chapter 7.

BECOMING AN ASSERTIVE COMMUNICATOR

If you have not had the best role models for building communication skills, you are not alone. A great majority of people have not had them either. The simple fact that you're reading this book is an indication that you're willing to learn something different, something that could potentially improve how you relate to others, and most importantly your partner. All of the communication techniques that I will provide in this book could help you not only with your partner, but also with friends, family, co-workers, and anyone that you come in contact with. Practice is very important when you are learning something new, so practice as much as possible with anyone you interact with on a daily basis. This is the only way that you will gain confidence to use these techniques, and actually remember to use them with your partner in a moment of disagreement or arguments. You can become an assertive communicator with practice and the proper motivation to do so. The following are techniques to help you become an assertive communicator:

Use **soft startups** to your conversation. Research suggests that 96% of the time, the way a discussion begins can predict the way it will end (Gottman & Silver 1999). If you start a conversation with a positive tone, it will most likely end on the same positive tone. Stay away from harsh startups such as accusations, negativity or contempt. For instance, if you begin dialogue with "Honey, I know that you're working hard to provide a better future for us," and then follow with your request to spend more time together, you can have a very different outcome than if you start your dialogue with "You're a workaholic who doesn't care about spending time with me." Paying attention to your tone of voice is important in your efforts to use soft startups. If you first recognize your partner's efforts, they'll be more likely to hear anything that you have to say next.

Use **"I" statements.** Thom Gordon first used the term "I messages" in the 1960s (Gordon 2000), and since then it has been used in programs for effective communication, in therapy, and in corporate training. Examples are phrasings such as: " I feel......," "I would like .....," "I thought........." These types of statements communicate ownership of your feelings, thoughts, and desires, instead of blaming or accusing others. The opposite of "I" statements are "you" statements: "you make me feel......," "you have to.......," "you are wrong ...." Using "I" statements can reduce perceived accusations as well as add a sense of personal agency and ownership to what you say.

Use **objective and descriptive statements,** especially when referring to the actions of your partner. This could look like: "I noticed that you forgot to take out the trash." These statements maintain the conversation around the facts that have taken place, without accusations or judgments. Using objective and descriptive statements can be a challenge since we live in a culture which motivates us to constantly judge, so it can take a lot of practice. Describing with words what you see and hear can help you practice objectiveness. It can also help you think about what is happening while it is happening, giving you time to act more effectively. The opposite of objective and descriptive statements are assumptions and judgments about your partner's actions and intentions.

Use **specific statements** when describing situations, thoughts, feelings and intentions. Stay away from extreme words like ALWAYS and NEVER. "I noticed that you left your dirty clothes on the floor a few days this week" is much less hurtful and presumptuous than "You always leave your clothes on the floor."

In order to better understand this, I usually ask my clients to think about a chore that they do not like to do such as washing the dishes. If you hate washing the dishes, but have done it a couple of times during the past month, the moment your partners says "you never wash the dishes," you will remember about those two times you washed the dishes and will try to defend the untruthful statement that was just made by your partner. Being specific also provides more information, reducing the need to fill in the blanks or make assumptions about what you're trying to communicate.

Take responsibility for your actions. We all make mistakes, and whether you like it or not, your partner will know it. Acknowledging when you make a mistake or even just owning up to your influence on a problematic situation can reduce the tension during an argument. Example: "I think we could work on being better communicators," instead of "You need to learn to communicate."

Use **tactful statements** and avoid name-calling. Example: "I disagree with that," instead of "That's stupid." You're probably tactful at work because you have to be. Guess what? If you're not tactful with your partner, they may feel disrespected or put down. Do you like to feel disrespected or put down? I don't think so. If you have the ability to be careful with what you say at work or in a professional setting, you can surely take the time to do the same with your partner.

Ask or request what you want from your partner, instead of demanding it or expecting them to know. Example: "I would like it if you could pick up the laundry from the drycleaners," instead of "you should pick the laundry from the drycleaners." Asking for what you want is your right. Of course there is no guarantee that you will get it because you cannot force anyone to do something that they do not want to do, but you can work at convincing your partner. Try to avoid using words like "should" or "have to" when asking for something, since these words communicate an obligation or command. Most individuals do not like to be told what to do, including yourself; your partner may have a negative reaction to your request when told that they "should" or "have" to do something.

Praise or recognize your partner's efforts specifically. A sentence like "it was nice of you to remember about my work presentation today" can go a long way towards making your partner feel appreciated. Recognizing what your partner does right (instead of only pointing out what is not happening or what you do not like) will most likely motivate them to do it again. I strongly recommend this technique for couples where partners feel unappreciated, as it can provide a great source of motivation for improvement in the relationship.

Show empathy towards your partner. Empathy is the ability to understand your partner's experience from their perspective, not yours. Example: "I can see that you're worried about money this month." Trying to understand your partner's feelings can go a long way when disagreeing or having different opinions. Even if you cannot agree on your differences, letting your partner know that you're trying to understand their point of view can demonstrate respect and caring. Showing empathy can determine the course of the conversation. I will tell you more about empathy and the impact it can have in your relationship in the next chapter.

Remember that all of these techniques are learned, and you can learn them too. Practicing them with your partner and others around you will help you become more confident to use them in a moment of tension, and more likely to remember them too. You do not have to use them all at once; depending on the situation you may use one or two. As you learn and practice these techniques, I suggest that you try one at a time by consciously introducing them into your conversations.

DESTRUCTIVE COMMUNICATION

Dr. John Gottman, a recognized expert in the field of couples therapy and psychology, has identified four prominent negative interactions between couples that are detrimental to marriages or committed relationships. He called them the *The Four Horsemen* (Gottman & Silver 1999).

1. **Criticism** is attacking the character of your partner instead of identifying negative behaviors (observing and describing). Calling your partner "selfish" or "lazy" are examples of criticism. This is also called labeling, which is naming your partner for their actions. Criticism can lead to much conflict, since your partner isn't defined by their behavior. If you called your partner "lazy" because they didn't want to wash the dishes after dinner, your partner may take offense since they cleaned the house that afternoon, or had a long day at work. More than anything, criticism is perceived as a direct attack by you on your partner about what he or she does wrong, or fails to do.

2. **Contempt** refers to the feeling that your partner is not worthy of any respect, which comes from a position of superiority, and usually follows criticism. Name-calling, eye rolling, sarcasm,

and hostile humor are usual expressions of contempt. This type of interaction makes your partner feel belittled. It sends the message that you feel superior.

3. **Defensiveness** is the reaction to feeling attacked by your partner. Defending your innocence, meeting an attack with a counterattack, and denying responsibility for a problem are all examples of defensiveness. Unfortunately, acting in a defensive manner will not help you solve any problems it only creates more. You may believe that you have good reasons to act defensively, especially if your partner is criticizing you or expressing contempt towards you, but acting defensively can sometimes make the situation worse because it leads to an escalation of the situation.

4. **Stonewalling**, tuning out, or ignoring your partner will usually follow the previous interactions, and leads to your partner feeling ignored and angrier. Stonewalling leads to the engages-distance or mutual-avoidance negative cycles of interactions discussed in Chapter 2. In addition, it can communicate to your partner that you do not care about what he or she has to say, which creates frustration and disappointment.

When combined over time, these four common interactions can lead a couple to consider and even seek divorce. Criticism, contempt, and defensiveness are forms of aggressive communication, while stonewalling is a form of passive-aggressive communication. Learning effective communication can help a couple communicate their needs and desires in a safer interaction.

Peter and Erica came into therapy reporting struggles to communicate. After their initial assessment, it was confirmed that they had difficulty expressing their desires and needs and they both engaged in destructive communication. As a result, they felt frustrated and discouraged. Here is what their dialogue sounded like:

> Erica: When are you going to find a real job?
>
> Peter: I'm looking, but I've no luck. People won't give me a chance (defensiveness). I've been getting by with little jobs here and there.
>
> Erica: I'm tired of hearing excuses, you're just plain lazy and irresponsible (criticism). I'm the one having to worry about bills. Start acting like a man (contempt).
>
> Peter: You're a jerk (contempt). It's not my fault that I'm overqualified (defensiveness).
>
> Erica: Why am I wasting my time? I can't deal with you anymore (contempt).
>
> Peter: Whatever you say (stonewalling).

As you can see, in the previous dialogue, nothing got resolved. Both Peter and Erica are feeling disappointed from each other and hurt. After learning about the effect of the *The Four Horsemen*, they became more aware of the impact that their words had on each other. My suggestion is to practice awareness of your interactions with your partner. Thinking about what and how you're going to say something can absolutely make a difference in your communications, as well as overall interactions.

Questions that can help you reflect or assess if you're engaging in destructive communication:

- Are you or your partner engaging in criticism?
- Are you or your partner expressing contempt?
- Are you or your partner acting defensively towards each other?
- Are you or your partner stonewalling while one brings up an important issue?

Remember, if you're not aware of your actions while interacting with your partner it will be difficult to change what is not working for you. The first step is awareness.

ACTIVE LISTENING

As mentioned earlier, one of the major issues causing couples to seek professional help is their difficulty with communication, particularly their listening skills. This prevents couples from understanding each other and, even more importantly, from solving problems or compromising. Therefore, the same problems keep coming up time after time. Keep in mind that most people do not learn to communicate effectively. Listening is a major portion of communication. In my experience, active listening is one of the most important communication skills. Here are some basic active listening techniques that I usually teach couples who are seeking to improve their communication:

- **Clarifying**: Asking questions to help you understand what your partner is trying to say. Example: "Are you saying that I insulted you?" This technique can be important in your efforts to avoid assumptions or misunderstanding.
- **Restating**: Restating your understanding of what is being said with facts (describing observations) or the basic idea of what is being communicated. Example: "Just so I understand, you're saying that I called you at a busy time yesterday?" Taking this extra step in your communication efforts can also help you avoid assumptions and misunderstandings.
- **Encouraging**: Showing interest in what your partner is saying by using neutral words and a neutral tone of voice in an effort to encourage him or her to continue talking. Examples: "Go on…." "O.K." "Uh huh." Encouraging demonstrates that you

care about what your partner feels and thinks, and that you're paying attention.

- **Summarizing**: Reviewing the progress of the conversation by restating major ideas, and establishing a basis for further discussion. Example: "It sounds like you're frustrated at work because your boss is giving you extra responsibilities?" This technique shows you were paying attention to what was said, and even better—that you're trying to understand.

- **Validating**: Acknowledging your partner's feelings, efforts and worthiness. Example: "It sounds like you put a lot of effort into finishing your project at work." This is one of THE most important active listening techniques, so important that I want to further explain the impact of validation in the next chapter.

- **Reflecting**: To reflect your partner's basic feelings as you understand them. Example: "You seem sad about your friend moving to a different town." Reflecting is useful in your efforts to validate.

Remember Peter and Erica? Let's see how their conversation could have turned if they used active listening skills.

Erica: When are you going to find a real job?

Peter: I'm looking, but I've no luck. People won't give me a chance. I've been getting by with little jobs here and there.

Erica: What do you mean by people are not giving you a chance? (clarifying)

Peter: I've gone to interviews and talked to people, but I don't seem to get hired. I'm starting to question if there is something that I am doing.

Erica: You sounds discouraged (reflecting).

Peter: I am. I'm not sure what else I need to do.

Erica: You're saying that you've gone to interviews and talked to people about getting a job, but nothing has come out of it (summarizing).

Peter: "Uh huh" (encouraging).

Erica: Let's figure something out. Maybe we can work on a new strategy for you to use in interviews. The truth is that I'm starting to worry about bills, our savings are running out quickly.

Peter: I can see why you're worried (validating), our lifestyle has changed since I lost my job. I think that I'm overqualified for some of these positions; maybe I could work on my resume.

Erica: Maybe. I can help you if you want.

Peter: I'll work on it tonight and let you look at it.

In this alternative version of Peter and Erica's conversation, they seemed more willing to listen and understand one another, which lead them to work together in helping Peter figure out why is he not being hired. Ultimately, even if it didn't solve the entire problem, it created a stepping-stone for them to work together and motivate immediate action.

It's important to mention that all communication skills can be challenging to put into action because our feelings about a situation can get in the way of our efforts to be an effective communicator. Chapter 7 will show you some techniques to help you work with your emotions during a moment of tension or conflict. Not being able to regulate your emotions can make it almost impossible to apply all of the techniques that you learn.

In order to accomplish effective communication there are a few details that I want you to keep in mind. First, be mindful of your tone of voice, body language, and facial expressions, since these are also forms or communication (which are at times unconscious). Secondly, picking a good time to talk has a huge impact on your ability to communicate or listen to your partner, and you can avoid possible distractions that may get in the way of your efforts (in other words, don't start a complex debate one minute before kickoff, or *The Walking Dead* season finale). Lastly, try to start a conversation on a positive note, such as how much you love and care about your partner. This could set the tone for what you have to say next.

All of these techniques can be useful for you, but remember that if you don't put them into practice you'll soon forget about them. Like anything—muscle strength, foreign languages, or math skills—it's "use it or lose it."

Chapter 5

EMPATHY & VALIDATION

"Empathy is really the opposite of spiritual meanness. It's the capacity to understand that every war is both won and lost. And that someone else's pain is as meaningful as your own."
—**Barbara Kingsolver**

Eduardo and Andrea came into therapy feeling discouraged because despite their efforts to communicate, it seemed like they couldn't do anything right. Andrea grew frustrated since it seemed like everything she said was wrong according to Eduardo. On the other hand, he was easily angered because it seemed that nothing that he did was enough for Andrea. Both Eduardo and Andrea were feeling invalidated, and they both had difficulty empathizing with each other. Their arguments became a power struggle about who was "right." The following was one of their initial arguments:

Andrea: Can't you just show me that you care? I'm tired of feeling insignificant in your life.

Eduardo: **Come on! You don't know what you're talking about.**

Andrea: This is what I mean. I'm trying to tell you how I feel and I can't even get a word out before you tell me I'm wrong.

Eduardo: **This is absurd.** I try to show you that I care all the time.

Andrea: **You're wrong! This is not how things are.** You ignore my call and texts and come home and fall asleep on the couch watching TV. Even on the weekends when I think that we're finally going to spend time together, you make plans to play golf with your buddies from work.

Eduardo: **Stop feeling sorry for yourself. At least** I'm working hard to give you all the nice things you have, instead of partying with other women. Plus, you make your own plans with the kids and don't include me.

Andrea: **You got it all wrong.** I only do that because I know you'll make plans without us. I have to make up for you being absent. How else are they going to feel important?

Eduardo: Are you saying that I'm a bad father? Let's not go there. You know what, I'm sick of hearing about this. I can't have this talk right now.

In this previous argument, both Eduardo and Andrea were invalidating, and they also struggle to empathize with each other. They both ended up frustrated and defeated since neither felt understood. Other examples of invalidation that are not included in the previous script are categorized below.

Telling others how to feel or minimizing feelings:

Don't worry.

Get over it.

Don't take everything personally.

You can't be serious.

It's not worth it.

Don't be sad/sensitive.

Telling others how to look:

Don't look so sad.

Don't make that face.

Smile!

Denying other's perceptions:

That is ridiculous.

That is not the way things are.

You got it all wrong.

I don't judge you.

You're being irrational.

Showing intolerance to what others are saying:

This is getting pathetic.

This is getting really old.

Empathy and Validation are both equally important in our relationships. I would like to distinguish both, and how they can work together to help you improve yours. **Empathy** is the ability to understand another person's experience from their perspective ("Empathy" 2014). Validation is communicating or expressing your understanding (empathy) and acceptance towards your partner (Fruzzetti & Iverson 2004). Some people may be naturally empathetic, but many have to learn to be empathetic. For instance, if you see someone cry, you'll probably feel sad for them, or want to console them. No one had to teach you to console who is crying, maybe you felt an urge to do so. On the other hand, if you're sitting in a restaurant trying to enjoy your dinner and there is a screaming baby next to you, you're more likely to be annoyed and have thoughts such as "Why can't these parents control their baby?"

If you have children maybe you learned how hard it can be for these parents to deal with a situation like that, knowing that many around are annoyed and looking at you, expecting you to do something while all of your attempts are failing. If you have experienced both sides, it may be easier to be empathetic, since you have felt different emotions as a result of the different situations.

You may not be able to experience everything that your partner has experienced, but it's still possible to understand where they're coming from. One way that you could try to do this is by identifying the emotion they're feeling about a certain situation. For instance, if your partner was fired—even though you may have never specifically experienced being fired before, you've probably experienced being rejected in some other kind of form. Thinking in terms of emotions may make it easier to empathize with your partner. Thinking back to the time when you felt a certain emotion could help you better understand where your partner is coming from, even if what he or she is saying or doing does not make much logical sense to you.

I want to clarify that showing empathy or validation does not mean that you agree with your partner about **why** he or she did something, or that they are allowed to actively hurt your feelings. Having empathy simply means that given your partner's personality, feelings, thoughts, experiences, and perception about a situation, you could understand why he or she thinks or does what was said or done. In other words that you can put yourself in your partner's shoes, with their life experience, not yours. This can be challenging, especially when there are many emotions involved, including being hurt by your partner.

Without empathy, relationships would be extremely difficult; having empathy towards others around us can help determine success in different aspects of life, from relationships to the workplace (Goleman 2005). Earlier in Chapter 3, I mentioned how empathizing with the one who hurt you is part of the process of forgiveness. More so, thinking about your partner's painful experiences, shortcomings, limitations and fears could help you relate to their actions, thoughts and feelings—even if you do not agree with the result caused by them.

Having empathy towards your partner can definitely help you decrease aggressive reactions towards them, but if you're not communicating this empathy, how can your partner know that you're at least trying to make this better? Empathy can be communicated in different ways, starting with a simple look, with a hug or even with a touch, depending on the situation and the environment that you're in. For instance, if you're having breakfast with your partner and in-laws; you hear your mother in-law say to your partner, "when are you going to start losing weight?" Maybe you are aware of your partner's efforts and difficulties in this area, so you may feel sad for your partner and even angry at your mother in law. A look towards your partner or grabbing their hand may communicate the empathy you feel in that moment without the need for any words. When you are the one in conflict with your partner it may take a more complex explanation to let them know how you feel. That's when validation comes into play.

Validation is the communication of empathy or understanding and acceptance for your partner. The benefits of validation have been identified as (Fruzzetti 2006):

- Enhances communication
- Soothes strong emotions during conflict
- Slows or reverses negative reaction
- Builds trust and closeness between you and your partner

- Establishes your efforts to be a respectful partner
- Enhances self-respect

WHAT IS VALID?

You may be asking yourself: how can I validate my partner if I disagree with them, or their interpretation of events? Keep in mind that validation is not saying that your partner is right and that you're wrong. It's simply letting your partner know that given the facts presented, you could understand why he or she arrived at that conclusion. Take a look at the following points to help you better understand what to validate (Fruzzetti 2006):

- Validation is about WHAT IS REAL for your partner. Regardless of opinions, what your partner feels or thinks is real for him or her; there is a reason for it in their mind. If your partner tells you that they feel frustrated about having to reschedule your date night, and you respond with "you shouldn't feel sad, we'll make it up in a couple of days," then despite your good-faith efforts to repair the situation, you're invalidating your partner's feelings because they already feel frustrated—and that is REAL. Reality is what is experienced, therefore, it is what it is--and if it wasn't, it wouldn't be.

- What your partner experiences under a particular circumstance is what anyone would think, feel, or want to do. For instance, if you're late and your partner doesn't know where you are because you have not talked all day, it's natural that they might worry. As a result they may call several times, or even call others who may know where you are if you do not respond. Many people would.

- Emotions--we all have them, positive and negative. Validating emotions is a sign of acceptance towards your partner, whatever those emotions are, and however they came about.

- Desires—regardless if it's possible or not, your partner has wants and desires. This will allow you to provide what your partner wants if possible, or console your partner if what he or she wants is not possible presently, or in the future. Learning about what your partner desires helps you know your partner more intimately.

- Beliefs and opinions are many times different from one individual to another. Validating your partner's opinions and beliefs can demonstrate respect for their being, whether you agree or disagree. What your partner thinks is real, so acknowledging it is also a way to decrease defensiveness in a given situation, especially if your partner is passionate about their opinion.

- Actions are important to validate, especially what your partner is doing right. We all like to be recognized for our efforts.

- Validating your partner's suffering shows caring, understanding, and acceptance. It shows your willingness to share a sad moment to help alleviate your partner's worries and anxieties, and make suffering a little easier.

SO HOW DO YOU VALIDATE YOUR PARTNER?

So far, you may have gained an understanding of the importance of validation and why it's worth working on. But how do you validate? Here are 7 steps that you can take to help you validate your partner (Fruzzetti 2006):

1. **Show that you're paying attention and listen actively.** Remember in Chapter 4 when I presented communication techniques? Among the active listening skills was validation. When you listen to what your partner is trying to say, you're demonstrating respect, but more importantly you're

showing that you care. Keep in mind that as you listen to your partner, judgments and defensiveness are going to work against your efforts, so try to stay mindful and objective as you listen. For example, if you partner is talking, avoid looking at the TV or checking your phone, since these simple actions can communicate that what your partner has to say is not important to you.

2. **Acknowledge your partner's experience**, what he or she is doing, saying, feeling, thinking, or wanting. This is especially important when you disagree with your partner, since this can increase the chances of them trying to understand your point as well. This can be done whether your partner approaches you about a situation, or if you observe something. For instance, if you notice that your partner is quiet and seems distant from you after work, you may say, "I noticed that you're quiet and thoughtful, you seem stressed. What's going on?" This can lead to further conversation about what your partner is experiencing.

3. **Ask questions to clarify your understanding**. In your efforts to validate your partner, it will be useful to really understand what your partner is trying to say—otherwise it may seem dismissive or insincere. Example: "Are you disappointed because I was late, or because I forgot to get the milk?" Asking questions can also help you avoid making assumptions and leaping to incorrect conclusions if you're not sure about what your partner is trying to communicate to you verbally (or nonverbally).

4. **Try to understand your partner's problems or mistakes in a larger context**. Try to empathize with the feelings and desires behind your partner's actions. For instance, if your partner impulsively quits their job after being miserable at work for months, you may (understandably) be pretty upset since his or her actions can be detrimental to the financial stability of

your household. Empathizing with your partner's feelings that led them to act impulsively does not mean that you agree with the consequences, but it may help you later discuss the impact of your partner's actions. Many times, if your partner makes a mistake or causes negative consequences that will impact you or the entire family, it's more likely that he or she already knows it and may be experiencing some guilt as a result. Assuming that your partner does not care about you or your family will create even more suffering for both of you, especially if it's not discussed. Validating your partner's experience can assist in transitioning from conflict to problem solving mode.

5. **Understand historical reasons for current experiences.** Try to think about all of the experiences that shaped your partner— good and bad—in an effort to try to understand their current reactions, even when it doesn't make any sense at all. Always try to assume the best and give the benefit of the doubt before you have a chance to ask questions to help you clarify your understanding. For example, if your partner is sensitive to negative feedback, try to remember what you know about your partner's past that leads to his or her reactions today. Maybe he or she grew up constantly being criticized by their parents, or was abused in some form. Remember, before making accusations, think back to your partner's past experiences.

6. **Find the "of course" in his or her experience.** At times your partner will act in ways that —though you may not like—still make sense, at least in a general context. If your partner has worked really hard on getting a promotion and they give the promotion to a colleague, that is bound to cause frustration for almost anyone.

7. **Allow yourself to be as vulnerable as your partner.** In moments of tension, both partners experience intense emotions. It can

be easy to give in to your protective or defensive instincts, but this will typically only make the situation worse. Allowing yourself to express your needs and feelings when your partner is also trying to do the same may help you to realize you both probably feel or want something very similar. For example, if your partner is asking to spend time with you, and you already have plans to go out with your friends—he/she may say, "I miss spending time together." Think about your own objectives and desires regarding your relationship. Most likely you also miss spending time with your partner, but because of work, routine, and schedules it may be difficult. If you simply say "me too" it could open up room for compromises, and lead to a productive discussion of when you *can* spend time together.

Remember, validation is a way to communicate empathy, but also acceptance towards your partner. When attempting to validate keep in mind that it doesn't have to be about solving a problem. Validation can be challenging in the midst of a disagreement with your partner. You may not see immediate results for your efforts, but maybe you can commit to try "The Validation Rule of Three" (Fruzzetti 2006). If you can find the willingness and courage to validate three consecutive times in the face of invalidation, your partner almost always will go off the "offensive" and their negative reaction to you will begin to subside.

After Eduardo and Andrea learned about the importance of validation and the steps necessary to validate each other, their conversations moved from frustration and defeat to understanding and acknowledgement. Here is what their later conversations sounded like:

Andrea: Sometimes I feel insignificant in your life, like you don't care.

Eduardo: What do you mean? Of course I care about you. I care so much.

Andrea: Do you?

Eduardo: Yes. I'm sorry that you feel that way. It's never my intention that you feel insignificant (validation). Maybe I need to work on showing you more often.

Andrea: I would like that.

Eduardo: I guess I think that you prefer spending time with the children instead of me.

Andrea: I like it when we spend time together as a family, but it's not the same as spending time you and I. Plus, since you're busy I feel like I have to overcompensate and give the children extra attention so they don't miss you.

Eduardo: That's understandable. Maybe we can all go to the beach this weekend and you and I can go out at night together.

Andrea: I like your plan. I'll get a babysitter.

Eduardo: Sounds good. I love you.

Other examples of validation might look like this:

I can see how you're *upset* about this.

I understand why you're disappointed.

You seem sad about this.

What a difficult situation.

I know how much this means to you.

That stinks.

How frustrating.

I hope that after reading these steps to help you validate your partner, you have a better idea of the importance of validation in your relationship. Remember that trying these techniques and experiencing the results they bring could help you maximize their effectiveness in your relationship. Practice, practice, practice is what will give you the confidence to get better at it.

WHAT HAPPENS IF YOU HAVE BEEN INVALIDATED FOR LONG PERIODS OF TIME?

This is a real question, since many individuals find themselves feeling invalidated for years, and may conclude that there is no turning back. It's understandable to feel unmotivated to make any changes to improve your relationship if you have been invalidated for a long period of time. More so, you may feel like nothing that you do or say is good enough for your partner due to this invalidation. Committing to make changes, as well as keeping a long-term goal of having a loving relationship where you both feel loved and supported could help you stay focused. During an argument, you may feel the urge to defend yourself from a perceived attack, but this will only create aggressiveness and feed into a loop of retaliatory attacks back and forward between the two of you. Thinking about why you're in a committed relationship with your partner (and his or her wonderful qualities) can help you stay focused in your efforts to validate each other and have the love and support you want from each other.

In your efforts to improve your relationship it's important that you learn to validate yourself, especially if your partner does not know how to validate you. The previous list presented in this chapter of how to validate your partner can also be used to validate yourself. If you expect your partner to validate you without learning to validate yourself, you will probably experience much disappointment and frustration, since there is no guarantee that your partner will want to (or learn to) validate you—but you can. In addition, if you can learn to validate yourself, it will be easier to learn to validate your partner since you'll get to practice.

Learning to accept things as they really are, and not necessarily as you want them to be, can help you move from frustration to effective problem solving. You may ask yourself "Why didn't my partner act differently?" "Why do I have to put in all the work?" "Why can't my partner do anything about it?" This type of thinking (especially asking yourself questions that you don't have an answer to, or you partner may not have an answer for) only keep you stuck in the hurt and suffering that has been caused. Try to stay focused on **what is** and **what you CAN do**, like the Serenity Prayer! In an ideal world your partner could have acted differently; he or she could put a lot work and effort towards your relationship, but that may not be the case and you may not be able to change this whether you like it or not.

CAN YOU REPAIR THE DAMAGE THAT HAS BEEN DONE?

The answer is Yes! First, and most importantly, you have to find the motivation to repair your relationship and to validate. Think about your end goal of having a loving, caring, and supportive relationship. Focus on the positive qualities that attracted you to your partner. You may have to think about these daily in order to retain your motivation. Knowing how and *when* to repair invalidation is also important. Keep in mind that:

- Repairing attempts during an argument can be challenging since there are many intense emotions that get in the way. Wait until your emotion has subsided to validate or make a repair from invalidation. I will further discuss emotion regulation in Chapter 7.
- Pick a good time, so other things won't distract you or your partner.
- Be specific about the situation that your want to repair.
- Be mindful about the impact invalidation had on you or your partner.

- Allow your partner to experience and express feelings about invalidation, even if you don't like it.
- Make a commitment to yourself and your partner to work on self-control.

Practice these validation techniques and be mindful of the results you obtain; as you practice these techniques remember the "rule of three" mentioned before, validate three consecutive times in the face of invalidation to obtain best results.

Chapter 6
WANTS AND NEEDS

"That's how they say it: He loves you in his own way. Well, what about my way? What if I need for him to love me in my way?"
—**Tammara Webber**, *Between the Lines*

W e all have things we want out of life—for others around us, for the future, but especially for our partners. As I mentioned before, most people have basic needs in relationships that usually fall under the categories of safety, security and connection. **Safety** needs are about more than just physical safety, they also encompass economic, social, vocational, and psychological aspects. If these are missing in your relationships it's more likely that you feel insecure and unprotected (Maslow 1987) in your everyday life (and in your relationship, naturally). **Security** needs are about trust in your partner, your relationship and your future together (adapted from the Attachment theory in Chapter 1). **Connection** needs are about bonding with your partner, sharing something, and togetherness. There is no one need more important than the other, it all depends on what your priorities are in a relationship. You and your partner may not share the same needs, but as long as you can learn and clearly define both of your needs, you can attempt to fulfill them. When your needs in a relationship are not met, you'll have a void. You may feel unhappy, and your relationship will be more vulnerable to indiscretions and affairs (physical or emotional).

Often times, I find individuals that do not know how to ask for what they want or need—perhaps because they have little experience receiving it, or maybe because they simply expect it. I'll talk more about expectation later in this chapter. Remember that your experiences in life are a factor in your ability to ask for what you want, as well as your personality. Here are some facts about wants or needs in relationships (Linehan 1993):

1. It is OK to want or need something from someone else.
2. You have a choice to ask someone for what you want or need.
3. You can cope with it if you don't get what you want or need.
4. The fact that someone says no to your request doesn't mean that you should have not asked in the first place.
5. If you didn't get your objective, that does not mean you didn't go about it in a skillful way (though it can be possible).
6. You can insist on your rights and still be a good person.
7. You can understand and validate another person, while still asking for what you want.

If you find yourself disagreeing with any of these statements you're probably experiencing distress within yourself and in your relationship. If you do not know how to ask for what you want (or feel incapable of asking), you may not feel loved or cared for by your partner. Interestingly, you may feel the same way if you ask for what you want and your partner is not capable of pleasing you. The difference is that in the latter, you're giving your partner the opportunity to please you--contrary to the former, where your partner may not know what you want. Think about this: your partner may be putting a lot of effort into pleasing you, but it may or may not work since they're going about it blindly. Needless to say, it is important that you learn to assert your needs in an effective manner—not too soft, not too strong. The following technique was designed by Marsha Linehan (1993) and it's a great technique that I teach my clients often.

Describe the FACTS about the situation.
Express your feelings and thoughts about the situation.
Assert your wants and desires.
Reinforce with consequences.
Stay mindful by avoiding distractions.
Appear confident.
Negotiate.

In my experience this is a very powerful technique that you can use when asking for what you want, or when you have to say NO to an unwanted request. Let's take a look at how to use this technique in a bit more detail.

DESCRIBING the facts of a situation is a great introduction to any conversation, since you're basing your request on actual events. I want to clarify that facts are not your opinions or feelings, which are also important (next step), but the events that have taken place. What was said and/or done, which prompted your request. Fact are not debatable, they're reality. It's not about *why*, it's *what took place*. Make sure you are objective and use non-judgmental statements. Example: "This is the third time this week that you have come home late."

EXPRESSING your feelings and thoughts about the situation by using "I" instead of "you" statements (refer to Chapter 4 on communication). Try to stay away from using anger and frustration when describing your feelings, since they usually communicate aggressiveness. Be mindful of deeper emotions, since anger and frustration are usually secondary emotions to hurt, disappointment, sadness, loneliness, fear, guilt, etc. Describe how you feel or what you believe about the situation. Do not expect your partner to read your mind. Example: "It's really hard for me when you stay late at work, I miss you so much. I understand that you have projects to complete; it's just difficult for me."

ASSERT what you want or need from your partner. Make sure you're specific, and give details and instructions about what you want. Your partner isn't telepathic; the more information you provide, the less room there will be for assumptions about what you want, and the better chance that you'll get it. Stay away from "should have". The objective is to get to the point and communicate in an assertive manner. Example: "I would like for us to spend more time together. Can we plan something for this weekend?"

REINFORCE by letting your partner know about the positive effects of giving you what you want or need. This is the most important step to this technique. Here, you're telling your partner how they could also benefit by doing what you're asking. It's like you're selling your idea. This step will make your request even more desirable and appealing for your partner. Example: "I'll feel better and **we** could feel closer after we spend some time together. Thanks for being understanding."

STAYING MINDFUL to your request means that you're focused on your request—and nothing else. Avoid recycling arguments from the past. You can ignore your partner's attempts to distract from your request; just start over by repeating facts, expressing feelings, asserting your wants, and reinforcing.

APPEAR CONFIDENT with your body language, facial expressions, and tone of voice. If you talk too low you may not sound confident. If you get too loud, you may sound upset. Make sure you keep eye contact and a straight posture.

Be willing to **NEGOTIATE** if your partner refuses to give you what you want. Use this step only if needed. Remember that there is no guarantee that you'll get what you want, but maybe you can still get some or part of what you want. Avoid having an "all or nothing" stance. Encourage your partner to be empathetic by asking: "What would you do if you were me?" or "How would you go about this?"

Just like any technique that you learn, you have to practice these to make sure that they work for you. The more you practice, the better you'll get at using the technique. I suggest that you try to use it by making small requests from others, not only your partner. Once you feel more confident using this strategy, you can use it for a more important request during a difficult situation.

EXPECTATIONS

At times expectations can be confused with wants and needs. Expectations and *wants* may look similar, but they're not. Expectations are a strong belief that actions or events **have** to take place, and if they do not happen it will be devastating. On the other hand, wanting is a desire that an action or event will take place. Expectations are less flexible than wants, since they usually narrow your options or possible outcomes for a situation. Expectations are an *"all or nothing"* approach to life, and that kind of thinking can bring about depressed and anxious feelings regarding your relationship, yourself and your future (see chapter 7 for more on black and white thinking).

Expectations can bring much disappointment, particularly when you believe that others share them or will share them in the future, but they do not or will not. This belief can bring feelings of hurt, frustration, stress, and even anger towards your partner. The more expectations you have of others, the greater the chances are that they will let you down. This statement can sound confusing and even strange for some, because it's a fairly common practice to have expectations of others, especially your partners. The reality is that you cannot make your partner do something; he or she must choose to do it. Would you prefer that your partner do something because they are obligated to do it, or because they want to please you as a result of the love they have for you?

So there is a difference between asking for what you want and expecting your partner to give you what you want because he or she "should." There is also a difference between what is a **priority** for you, and what is a priority for others. Expecting others to have similar priorities is a recipe for disappointment. In an effort to avoid further letdowns, hurt, stress, frustration, anger, and sadness, I suggest lowering some expectations, especially the ones that keep disappointing you time after time. Of course, this is easier said than done. Many people come to therapy in an effort to let go of their expectations and learn to identify the beliefs where these expectations are rooted. You can learn new ways to communicate your needs and desires from your loved ones without the expectation that causes feelings of hurt and anger.

Many times, your attempts to ask for what you want or desire are perceived by your partner as expectations. They may feel they have no other option than to give you what you want. Your partner may describe your request as controlling, bossy, or authoritarian, or like you're speaking to them as if they were a child. If your intentions are to ask for what you want, and you have noticed that your partner perceives your requests as orders, this may lead to aggressive responses or defensiveness. I suggest that you pay attention to your communication—at times, the words that you're using may be sending the message that your requests are orders. Words like *should, should not, have to, and ought to* communicate expectations. I suggest that you work on replacing these words with: prefer, like and want. As you read these words you may be thinking, "but that's what I mean!" and I believe this is the case. Unfortunately, you partner may not be seeing that, because he or she cannot see your intentions—they can only see actions (what is said or done). By avoiding commanding words and using the previous communication technique you can increase your chances of being perceived like you're making a request, instead of demanding that things have to happen a certain way.

The following is an example of a case where expectations were creating much disappointment and insecurity in a relationship:

Mark came in to an appointment because he was frustrated and felt unloved. He reported that his girlfriend of three months was very busy with work, friends, family, exercise, etc. He stated that when they first met she was not working, but that recently she became employed and things started to change. I asked if this was the first time this had happened in his relationships, and he replied no. Mark stated that he'd had one other serious relationship where the same thing happened. Apparently in the beginning of both relationships everything was great; they spent almost all their free time together and talked about the future together, but as time passed things quickly changed. All of a sudden, the relationship changed and he started feeling that he was investing his time and feelings into a relationship that was one-sided because he did not feel that his girlfriend was investing as much as he was. As I listened to Mark, I couldn't stop to wonder what kind of expectations he had for his partners. So I asked: What could his girlfriend do to let him know that she was invested in the relationship? Mark replied quickly, with a surprised look, that he would be happy if they just spent time together. When I asked Mark "how much time?" he was unsure of the answer, and later reported that at least one hour of quality time together per day would make him happier. Even though Mark's need to spend quality time would help him feel loved, the amount of time he expects may not be the same that his girlfriend can or will be able to give him. In this case, his girlfriend getting a job was a major priority for her, especially after being unemployed for a while. If you remember the needs in relationships that I mentioned earlier in this chapter, you may notice that Mark and his girlfriend seemed to have different needs. For her, safety seemed to be important, and for him it was connectedness. One is not more important that the other, but if you do not figure out what your partner's wants and needs are, how can you help fulfill them? If your partner does not know what your wants and needs are, how can she or he fulfill them? As I explained to Mark that it seemed he was expecting that his girlfriend place emphasis on his need to connect, he was not making it easy to support his girlfriend on her own needs. You can be an example for your partner, in the sense that if you're willing to respect and accept your partner's needs and help to fulfill them, your partner in turn may do the same for you. If you wait for your partner to take the first step, you may wait for a long time...but if you take responsibility and take the first step, you're moving your relationship towards change and improvement.

Chapter 7

EMOTIONS

*"I don't want to be at the mercy of my emotions. I want
to use them, to enjoy them, and to dominate them."*
—**Oscar Wilde**, *The Picture of Dorian Gray*

E motions are a never-ending part of our lives. They have always been there, and always will. Emotions play a big role in our lives, especially in our relationships. Remember the beginning of your relationship, and what it felt like when you went on your first date, your first kiss, the first time you had sex, the moment you fell in love? You probably felt excitement, nervousness, flirtiness, happiness, mostly positive emotions. As time goes by and you get to know your partner and their imperfections you may disagree and argue at times. The emotions that often result are anger, frustration, sadness, and guilt, also referred to as negative emotions. I want to clarify that emotions are not negative or positive. They're mostly described that way because of the comfort or discomfort they bring. You may like to feel happy and excited (positive), but nobody enjoys feeling sadness, anger, frustration, and guilt; hence the label of "negative."

I want you to think back about what you have learned about emotions during your life experiences: what have you been taught you should do, or not do? Did you even talk about emotions growing up? It is not uncommon to have been conditioned to avoid emotions altogether. Many individuals never really learned to talk about them or express them. What is certain is that you have emotions and that you experience them all the time. Here are some common myths about emotions that you may have internalized (Linehan 1993):

1. There is a "right" way to feel about every situation.
2. Letting others know that I'm feeling bad is weakness.
3. Negative feelings are bad and destructive.
4. Being emotional means being out of control.
5. Emotions can just happen for no reason.
6. Some emotions are really stupid.
7. All painful emotions are the result of a bad attitude.
8. If others don't approve of my feelings, obviously I shouldn't feel the way I do.
9. Other people are the best judge of how I am feeling.
10. Painful emotions are not that important and should be ignored.

The above statements are untrue. However, if you find yourself agreeing with any of these statements I encourage you to work on challenging it or proving this statement to be wrong, because it's probably causing distress within your own mind and in your relationship. Challenging statements that you believe to be true can be difficult, but learning to challenge these unrealistic expectations you have about yourself and others can make a measurable difference in how you feel about yourself and your partner. An individual's present perceptions, thoughts, assumptions, beliefs, values, attitudes, and philosophies can be rational or irrational, which can cause automatic emotional responses towards self and others (Beck, 2005; Ellis, 1973).

Your feelings are the direct result of your thoughts, beliefs or values (Beck 2005). For instance, if you are carrying heavy grocery bags and are trying to get into the house, but your partner notices it and help you, you may think "It's nice of him or her to do this" and as a result feel joyful or thankful. On the other hand if you think "this is the least he or she can do after I had to go to the store by myself," you may feel frustrated, annoyed, angry, etc. I would like to share with you some common negative thoughts that usually result in anxious or depressed feelings, and what they mean. The following chart was designed by Arthur Jongsma (2007), which I have adapted to reflect couple interactions:

Type of Thinking	Definition	Example	Feelings/ Emotions that result
Black and White	Viewing situations, people or self as entirely bad or entirely good, nothing in between.	Your partner tells you that they prefer you call during non-business hours. You think: "He/ She hates it when I call."	Sadness, Disappointment Frustration Hurt
Exaggerating	Making self-critical or other-critical statements that include extreme terms like never, nothing, everything, or always.	Your partner forgot to ask you about attending a work dinner. You think: "She never asks me in advance."	Frustration Unfairness Disappointment Pressure

Discounting	Rejecting positive experiences as not being important or meaningful.	Your partner compliments your looks. You think: "He says that to anyone."	Disappointment Sadness
Catastrophizing	Blowing expected consequences out of proportion in a negative direction.	Your partner says: "I'm having problems at work." You think: "She is going to get fired."	Fear Sadness Tension Pressure
Judging	Being critical of self or others with a heavy emphasis on the use of words like: should, have, ought to, must, have to, and should not have.	Your partner forgets to pick up the laundry at the dry cleaners. You think: "She should know better than that."	Disappointment Frustration Sadness
Mind Reading	Making negative assumptions regarding other people's thoughts and motives.	Thinking "I know that he is doing this to upset me."	Anger Frustration Hurt Sadness
Forecasting	Predicting events will turn out badly.	Thinking "I know she will be upset."	Hurt Disappointment Sadness Fear
Feelings are facts	Because you feel a certain way, reality is seen as fitting that feeling.	Your partner has not brought up plans for the weekend. You think: "She must think that I'm boring."	Sadness Loneliness Hurt

| Labeling | Calling self or others a bad name when displeased with a behavior. | Your partner did not wash the dishes. You think: "He is so lazy." | Frustration Disappointment Annoyance Irritation |

These types of thinking affect the way you feel about yourself and others. For the purposes of this book I'm focusing on the impact that these thinking patterns have on your partner and your relationship. I encourage you to pay close attention to your thoughts about your partner and see what kinds of feelings are resulting. If you notice that most of your thoughts are negative and you are having negative feelings or emotions as a result, try to work on creating positive thoughts towards your partner and see how this can change your feelings. One way to practice changing your thoughts about your partner from negative to positive is by thinking about one thing that your partner is doing that you're grateful for. If you can think of more than one thing, great, but if you can only come up with one, that's fine too--as long as you're practicing.

EXERCISE

1. List three examples of your own thoughts that lead you to feel angry, frustrated, or sad towards your partner.
   A. What happened? (Think about the facts of the situation)
   B. What were the negative thoughts you had about the situation?
2. After identifying the negative thoughts about the situation, replace them with a more realistic, positive thought that can help you feel better towards your partner. Refer to the examples from above.
   A. What happened?
   B. Replacement positive thoughts

EMOTIONS DURING CONFLICT

It has been documented that as humans we have a "fight or flight" reaction (also described as freeze, fawn response, hyperarousal, or acute stress response), a physiological reaction that occurs in response to a perceived dangerous or harmful event, attack, or threat of survival (Cannon 1967). Even though during an argument with your partner you may not be under physical or harmful attack per se, it's the perception of being under attack that creates this instinctual reaction that is physiological in nature. This reaction creates much difficulty in your attempts to solve a situation, and subsequently makes things worse.

Think back to a difficult situation or disagreement with your partner. As previously mentioned it's natural for your emotions to become intense and overwhelming. This experience is also called *flooding* (Ekman 1984), which refers to an internal state of feeling overwhelmed by a partner's negative emotions or one's own emotions as the partner brings up issues. This makes it almost impossible to avoid becoming defensive, repeating oneself, or wishing to flee the situation (Gottman 2011).

I want you to visualize the last time that you had a disagreement with your partner—a time when either you or your partner introduced a difficult situation that lead to a disagreement. The moment that you heard your partner say something incorrect about you or your character, you most likely had a need or urge to do something about it. A recent theory also explains that emotions motivate or prepare us for action (Brehm 1999), which explains the need to act or do something as a result of intense emotions. In addition, human emotion can be motivated automatically without the involvement of conscious guidance or choice (Bargh 1990), which makes sense given that many actions taken as a result of emotion seem to happen without thought. Each emotion has different urges, and here are examples:

Anger: attacking verbally or physically, defending, yelling, throwing things, etc.

Sadness: staying in bed, crying, isolating, talking little, moving slowly, etc.

Guilt: withdrawing, hiding, avoidance, apologizing, trying to repair damage, etc.

Fear: Fleeing or running away, hiding, talking less, freezing, crying, shakiness, etc.

These responses to emotions are instinctive, such as the fight or flight discussed earlier, but you do not have to act on these urges. Ultimately, you have a choice to act despite strong urges. Think about times when you felt an urge to scream, but you didn't because it was inappropriate to the place. This is an example of your ability to choose your actions regardless of the emotional urge you felt.

Strong emotions like anger and frustration can help you overcome obstacles in your mind and your environment. Your emotional reactions to other people and to events can give you information about a situation. Emotions can be signals or alarms that something is happening. However, this is only an alarm, not proof that something is happening (unless you obtain more information that demonstrates this is a fact). Nonetheless, your urge to act is immediate even though it's only a signal. Remember, emotions are not facts—they're signals for you to find out more information about a situation.

Another important aspect about emotions is that they're temporary. They vary in intensity from low to high, and from high back down to low. It's simply a matter of time before an intense emotion subsides. Sometimes time is all you need to help you get a grip on your actions. During an argument, anything that you say or do can impact the situation for better or for worse. Being aware of your actions is important since they can determine the outcome of the situation. If you experience an intense emotion, it's more likely that you will act impulsively, because intense emotions and the urges they bring can be powerful. It also may seem like they control your actions, but they don't. You have control, even if it may not feel like it.

Here are some tips to help regulate an intense emotion during an emotional situation:

- Take a "time out" if your emotions are reaching a high point. Taking a break during an argument can help you clear your mind and rethink the situation, clarify your points and reconsider what your partner is saying.
- Wait. Waiting to bring up a difficult situation can help you in the same way as taking a break. Since all emotions are temporary, waiting until the intensity of your emotions come down will give you time to gather information to present your point of view or opinion about a disagreement.
- Go for a walk or get some kind of exercise. Physical activity is a great reliever of anger and frustration.
- Place a limit on your arguments. Talk to your partner about setting a time limit for your arguments. You both have to agree to enforce this rule.
- Breathe deeply and pay attention to your breathing. This exercise can be very effective in helping to calm down your heart rate and slowly decrease the intensity of your emotion.
- Stay focused on your objective. It's easy to get side tracked during an argument. Try to stay away from past arguments, or other situations that have nothing to do with the original point you were trying to make. Choose one objective at the time to help your partner better understand what you're trying to say. Too many things can be confusing and bring more emotions to the table.

Being able to regulate your emotions during an argument or disagreement is imperative in your ability to communicate and act in a favorable manner towards your partner. It's also important that you take regular steps to reduce the likelihood of negative emotions (e.g. anger, guilt, sadness) and the urges that come with them. Here are some steps you can take to maintain a healthy emotional state (Linehan 1993):

- **Treat any physical illness.** If you experience pain or any symptom of an illness you'll more likely be vulnerable to stress. For instance, if you have a headache, any loud noise is going to be bothersome. It's not the best idea to enter any serious discussion if you're experiencing any pain or illness— your body and emotional state will most likely work against your efforts.

- **Balance your eating.** Think about how easily you can get upset if you have not had anything to eat all day. Replenishing your body with the necessary nutrients it needs to function is imperative to help you deal with difficult situations. So do not bring up anything difficult if you're hungry and have not eaten.

- **Being under the influence of substances** such as alcohol and drugs (legal or illegal) impairs your ability to reason or evaluate possible consequences for your words, actions, and expression of emotions. Staying away from intoxicating substances is imperative to your efforts.

- **Getting the sleep** your body needs is important for your physical and mental health, as well as your ability to deal with stress. Think about how hard it can be to get through your day if you didn't sleep well the night before. So make sure you get your sleep, and if you don't, it's probably not a good time to talk about difficult situations.

- **Create more positive experiences**. Often situations entirely outside of your control can cause you to feel sad, but you can create positive experiences for yourself, even if you don't really want to. Push yourself and make an effort to create positive events with the ones you love. This can help you balance the negative events (which you have limited control of) with positive events in your life.

Two months after moving to a new house, I was tired, overwhelmed and frustrated with what seemed the never-ending task of unpacking. This particular day, I didn't get a full night sleep the previous night and I had been working in the yard all morning and early afternoon. My husband brought up his own frustration with the clutter around the house weeks after the move.

> My husband: I'm tired of the house being a mess. Can you just get rid of some of the clutter and keep this place organized?
>
> Me: (My mind started racing with thoughts and memories about everything that I had done to get the house organized after the move. I started feeling unappreciated and hurt that my effects were not recognized.) I'm constantly trying to do something to keep the house organized. It feels like a never-ending battle to pick up after Lucas (our 2 year old son) and work on getting the house organized. If you helped me more with him, I would have time to work around the house.
>
> My husband: What are you talking about? (invalidation) I just watched Lucas and fed him while you were working outside. It doesn't take much to look after him.
>
> Me: Yes, you did it today, but I'm talking about the rest of the week (invalidation). - At this time I felt overwhelmed

with emotions about thoughts and assumptions that I was not doing enough.

My husband: What about me cleaning the gutters, organizing the garage and watching Lucas while you work late? All after I come home from working all day, but it's never enough for you, nothing that I do is enough.

We ended the conversation due to the intense emotions we were both experiencing, which were only creating more hostility and not leading us to a productive place. I then took a shower, and my husband also took a shower. This helped us both to relax and helped me reflect on the argument. I realized that we were both tired and feeling unappreciated for our efforts. I also didn't get enough sleep the night before and had been working on the yard for a great portion of the day, so my mind and body were depleted. I rested for the remainder of the day, and later that night I approached my husband with the conversation that we started earlier.

Me: I appreciate everything you do around the house (validation). I'm sorry that you felt unappreciated; my intention is not for you to feel that way. We both have been working really hard to get the house unpacked and organized. I feel frustrated too; It's hard to accept that this is a process. It's going to take time to find places for all of our stuff. I think that we have been socializing and going out a lot this past week so we have not really had time to work in the house.

My husband: Yes, we need to keep the socializing to a minimum for a while. Let's not go anywhere next weekend so we can work on the house.

Me: O.K. I don't have a problem with that.

My husband: I just want the house to look organized, even if it's not all unpacked. I don't like clutter. Let's organize what we have out tomorrow instead of continuing unpacking.

Me: Sounds good.

Taking that break during the argument kept us from continuing becoming more hostile and aggressive towards each other. It also helped me become mindful of my emotions and reflect on my thoughts, assumptions and vulnerabilities. My husband was able to listen to my efforts to validate his feelings and clarify my intentions, which led us to focus on a solution.

As part of your efforts to improve your relationship, I encourage you to be mindful of your own emotions, since they directly impact your ability to communicate and apply all of the techniques you will learn in this book. Remember, emotions are temporary, and you will eventually feel better. Try not to hold on or suppress emotions, even if they're uncomfortable. Instead, try to accept your emotion so you can move on to figure out what is causing you to feel it (signaling), and the facts about situations that lead you to feel a certain way. If you find yourself making assumptions about your partner's actions or intentions which are creating negative feelings, you can try to practice some of the communication techniques that I covered in Chapter 4, such as clarifying and asking questions in order to prove your assumptions correct or incorrect.

As you can see, so far emotions have a direct impact on your ability to deal with a situation. That goes double for arguments, since you cannot help but feel intense emotions during one. It's important that you can learn to deal with powerful emotions during an argument since this kind of self-control can make a major difference in how effective your communication can be.

Chapter 8

PROBLEM SOLVING
& COMPROMISING

art of the reason that relationship conflicts continue to happen time after time is that the issues do not get fully resolved, or the couple is not able to reach a compromise. JP and Alex came to see me after years of unresolved conflicts. They were both frustrated and fed up with their situation, but more so they both thought they were trying to make things better--and getting no results. They both grew up with critical and negative parents, which led both to learn to avoid conflicts all together, each in a different way. More importantly, they had not learned the skills to address conflicts, so they didn't. Here is what their interaction sounded like:

> Alex: Can you meet me, and the kids for lunch after I pick them up from school?
> JP: O.K.

Alex: Great. Lately you seem distracted around the kids. Please ask them about their day and interact with them.

JP: You know what, I do what I can. I'm busy at work, but I'm trying to make time for all of you. If you don't like it, then let's not go.

Alex: Fine. I'll go with the kids alone. It's like I'm a single mom. We're used to being without you anyway.

JP: If that's what you think, why do you even ask me? I don't have time for this.

Alex: You never have time for anything.

Problem solving and compromising are two sets of skills needed in order to fully implement many of the concepts in this book. More so, *agreement* is one of the four common themes that are important to relationship quality (Hassebrauk & Fehr 2002). Now, I would like to clarify that the objective of this chapter is not to convince you that you and your partner have to agree on everything, but to learn to solve problems that may be limiting the quality of your relationship (if they can be solved), and also to learn to compromise in an effort to accept each other's differences (agree to disagree). Once again, I want to point out that these skills are usually learned throughout life (like many behavioral patterns mentioned in this book) by the examples somebody had around, or the experiences lived in their life. The importance of learning problem solving skills has been recognized by many, and so guidelines and programs have been created that apply to a great variety of situations. In this chapter I will refer to these skills in terms of your romantic relationship, but I want you to know that they can be used in any situation, anytime you're interacting with someone.

Think back to chapters one and two and the avoidance that some individuals experience. Some people avoid conflict because they fear getting hurt or hurting their partners. In fact, some know from experience that arguments with their partners will end up that way; the two start to disagree, the disagreement escalates and then "blows up." Meanwhile, nothing gets resolved (Gottman, Gottman, & Declaire, 2007). What happens next is called the *Zeigarnik effect*, which is based on the belief that our ability to recall unfinished tasks is superior to the recall of completed tasks (Zeigarnik, 1927). In relationships, this phenomenon is demonstrated when a couple's negative interactions are not fully processed or resolved, then instead are remembered and rehearsed repeatedly, turned over and over in each person's mind (Gottman 2011), to the point that it may seem obsessive for you or your partner. You may have said or heard phrases like "why can't you just let things go?" or "you said that you were going to _____."

Avoiding the Zeigarnik effect is accomplished by fully processing a negative event. In this case that means solving the problem, compromising, "being there" for your partner or your relationship, and demonstrating that you have your partner's best interests in mind. If you're able to successfully implement these steps, you or your partner can potentially forget about the hurt or minimize the negativity in your relationship (Gottman 2011). Talking about conflicting differences with your partner can be an emotional discussion, especially if you feel strongly about your point of view. The following guideline was designed by John and Julie Gottman (2007), as a blueprint for handling conflict. Try following these steps when talking about conflictive subjects:

1. Set aside a quiet time to discuss one single conflict at length.
2. Designate one person as the speaker and one person as the listener.
3. The speaker begins talking about the conflict, saying everything they want to say about their point of view (use assertive communication skills from Chapter 4). The speaker uses "I messages" and avoids "you" statements. The listener can ask

questions and take notes. Writing things down gives the speaker the distinct feeling that what they're saying really matters to the listener. When the listener asks questions, those questions are simply to ensure understanding. The listener *must* delay talking about solutions and postpone any attempts to try to persuade the speaker. The listener can't use questions to imply his or her disagreement. The listener should not present his or her own view. The listener's job is simply to listen (use active listening skills from Chapter 4). The whole interaction should be civil and polite.

4. When the speaker is completely finished, the listener restates the speaker's point of view. The speaker listens carefully and clarifies anything the listener didn't really seem to understand. Then the listener restates the position. This process repeats until the speaker is satisfied that the listener really understands.

5. Switch roles and start over with step 1.

One of the objectives of this guideline is listening and validating feelings. Express everything that you have to express about your viewpoint and postpone persuasion until your partner also has a chance to express his or her viewpoint. (See Chapter 4 & Chapter 5 for more techniques on listening and validating). By allowing for expression and listening to each other despite your differences, you're creating better understanding, emotional connection, and respect—even if you do not agree on the subject. An important factor in following this guideline is your ability to regulate intense emotional arousal (see Chapter 7), otherwise it would be extremely difficult to follow these steps, or even attempt to find solutions. Gottman (2011) found that in relationship conflicts, people do not always act rationally. This was related to each individual's inability to regulate their emotional intensity and calm themselves.

Compromise is usually understood as finding a middle ground between you and your partner. Compromising comes with an implicit sense of fairness, which is where things can get complicated since fairness can be perceived differently. Your idea of what is fair may not be your partner's. The following steps were created by Janet Hibbs and Karen Getsen (2009), and can be key elements to help couples reach fairness and compromise:

1. Rethink your expectations about what is fair. Considering your partner's perception of what is fair will help you reach a realistic compromise. Maybe your expectations are too high for your partner, which will make it unlikely that he or she will actually live up to them, leading to great disappointment for you.

2. Ask for what you need, and ask your partner to clarify what he or she needs. Ask: What are your needs here? What do you wish for? In order to try to find a middle point it's important that you have a clear view of what is wanted. Read between the lines and seek clarification of what is understood. Try to stay away from what is *not* happening or what you don't like. For instance, say "I want to hear from you throughout the day. I want you to call me," instead of "You obviously don't care about me since you never call me."

3. Show appreciation for what is being done or for efforts being made. Appreciation goes a long way in motivating new efforts and actions. We all like to be acknowledged or recognized for what we do or try to do. Showing appreciation is one way of positive reinforcement for desired behaviors. The more you show appreciation for a behavior, the more likely the behavior will take place in the future.

4. Change the rules. Life is ever-changing so adapting to life changes and your individual growth will also serve a purpose for

compromising and being fair in your relationship. Flexibility and adaptability are possibly the greatest capabilities we have as human beings in order to survive.

Ideally, the goal of compromising is to achieve a win-win situation between you and your partner. In order to achieve this goal you'll probably need to be able to negotiate your request or your partner's request. Remember the communication technique from Chapter 6? That technique provides a way to negotiate your request by asking: What would you do if you were me? This creates the opportunity to have your partner stand in your shoes, or vice-versa. Negotiation is a form of flexibility, since it'll usually allow for you to get some (or more) of what you want, instead of not getting anything at all.

I've said it before and I'll say it again, being in a relationship is not about you winning or losing, since I see many times that the need to win an argument gets in the way of effectiveness. Your own or your partner's supposed "wins" may corrode your relationship over time, and your relationship will become unbalanced. Impulsivity, insecurities, fears, and pride, to name a few, are usually behind the need to win. Think in terms of your relationship winning, as in "what is best for my *relationship*?" When you place your relationship as a priority in an argument or disagreement, it can be easier to negotiate, be fair, and ultimately compromise. Otherwise, it can be an uphill battle to fight, because winning and compromising can work against each other.

EMOTIONAL CLOSENESS DURING CONFLICT

During conflict, emotions tend to rise to the surface, varying in intensity. At times these emotions blind us to logic or reason (See Chapter 7). Therefore, using an emotional closeness approach can help you reach your partner in a different way in the heated moment of the conflict. Think about how many times you have had a disagreement about something that made no logical or reasonable sense to you, but it made plenty of sense to your partner (or the other way around). It's important to be aware of your emotions during conflict, since they can either motivate destructive or positive interactions. Furthermore, research suggests that repair attempts based on emotional closeness (taking responsibility, agreement, affection, humor, self-disclosure, understanding, and empathy) are highly effective (Gottman 2011). Try to avoid logic-based approaches, since research tends to show that logic-based repairs in couples are quite ineffective (Gottman 2011). Let's take a look at the attempts that have been identified as emotional closeness in more detail:

Taking responsibility - Accepting that you have contributed something to cause or maintain a situation, even if you had only a small part, can take a certain level of maturity. It can also reflect the respect that you have for your partner. Don't let pride get in the way of taking responsibility for your actions, either intentional or unintentional; taking responsibility for your actions can help your remember that we all make mistakes from time to time, and to be humble. It also helps you move from "I win" mode to "we win" mode.

Agreement - Agreement can be the source of the problem, since you cannot agree on a specific subject, but think about the facts of the situation—not your own or your partner's opinion about how and why things happened. Facts could be the one thing that you could agree on. Even if it's the only thing, it may be better than nothing.

Affection - Showing affection during conflict may be difficult to imagine, since many times our need to defend ourselves urges us to keep a distance and avoid interaction with our partners. I encourage you to act opposite to this urge and make yourself be affectionate, but if this is too much or too difficult for you, you can still show affection in other ways—such as doing alternative things that you usually do out of love towards your partner (see Chapter 9) for different ways to demonstrate love.

Humor - Interestingly, research has established that humor during couples' conflict interaction is effective in reducing physiological arousal (Levenson & Gottman, 1985). Remember Chapter 7 and the importance of regulating emotions during conflict? Humor can be used to decrease tension. Now, I would like to make it clear that I'm not talking about sarcasm or ridiculing your partner, but using humor to change the tone of the interaction in a way to diffuse negativity. By using humor you can be less defensive in your reactions, and even allow for deeper emotions to surface. When using humor during conflict, it's important to be clear that you're not making fun of your partner—instead you're either laughing at yourself or both of you. Being aware of your partner's sense of humor will be crucial since the humor needs to be shared, otherwise it defeats the purpose. Another important factor is that you don't hide your emotions behind humor, since expressing your emotions can help your partner understand how the situation disputed is important to you and how it's affecting you. Example: Share a funny story related to the problem, or make fun of yourself (again, not in a sarcastic manner) for your shortcomings.

Self-disclosure - Expressing your own feelings, thoughts, motivations, and ideas about a situation is central to promoting problem solving. Otherwise, your partner may be blind to your needs and act in ways that would continue to deeply hurt you. You can also use self-disclosure to share a time when the roles were reversed—not for the purpose of avoiding taking responsibility, or revenge, but to help your partner understand your position or feelings.

Understanding - By making attempts to understand your partner's logic or reasoning behind his or her actions, you could demonstrate caring. Try to put yourself in your partner's shoes with his or her life experience, not yours. This attempt will lead to expressing the validation mentioned earlier (See chapter 5), and it will help you in your relationship, especially during conflict with your partner.

Empathy - The difference between understanding and empathy is that the second focuses on emotional understanding, not just logic and reasoning. Being able to empathize with your partner is very important in a relationship, so much that Chapter 5 of this book is dedicated to understanding and expressing empathy.

The following are questions and statements that can help you communicate emotional closeness:

What are you feeling?
What else are you feeling?
What are your needs here?
What do you wish for?
Who are the main characters in this thing?
How did this all evolve?
Talk to me, I am listening.
We have lots of time to talk.
Tell me your major priorities here/in this situation.
Poor Baby!
I know what that feels like.
I can see/understand why you're so upset.

Let's go back to JP and Alex and see how their conversation would have sounded if they used emotional closeness during their interaction:

Alex: Can you meet me, and the kids for lunch after I pick them up from school?
JP: O.K.
Alex: Great. Lately you seem distracted around the kids. Please ask them about their day and interact with them.

JP: I have been distracted lately (taking responsibility). I'm working on this project at work and I'm feeling stressed about it. I did notice that I haven't dedicated much time to you or the kids in the last couple of weeks (agreement).

Alex: I noticed that you have been stressed (validation/understanding). I know what that feels like (empathy). Remember when I had to go to California for a month?

JP: Yeah.

Alex: That was difficult for all of us. I felt so guilty leaving you and the kids alone. I remember that hardest part coming back, it took Vickie a couple of minutes to recognize me and hug me (self-disclosure).

JP: That was hard. I remember that after that she held on to you like a leech (humor?), even when you wanted to shower she was there.

Alex: *smile*

JP: Honey, I love you and miss you (affection).

Alex: Me too. I just want our family to be closer. Is there anything that I can do to make things easier for you?

JP: I like it when we meet for lunch after you pick up the kids. Maybe you can come by more often.

Alex: I can try to do that.

JP: I can try to be more present too. Maybe I can take a couple of days off next week and we can get out of town for a while.

Alex: That sounds great. Let's try spending time together.

After JP took responsibility and Alex showed understanding and empathy, the conversation went on smoother than the previous one. Applying emotional closeness during conflict can go a long way towards your efforts to find a solution to a specific situation. It can also help you demonstrate the care and affection you feel for each other even in a moment of tension. Everything that you do or say during conflict becomes facts in the history of your relationship. Try practicing this approach of emotional closeness and find out what kind of results it brings for your life.

PROS AND CONS

When debating back and forth with your partner about solutions or options to solve a situation, you can work together despite your differences. One way is not better than the other, despite our initial beliefs. I've come to find out that very rarely do problems have one solution. One way that you can help your partner see the benefits of your suggestions and vice-versa, is to work together. Here is a problem solving technique that you can follow (Jongsma, 2007):

1. Describe the problem of conflict between you and your partner in as much detail as possible. Allow your partner to do the same.

2. Brainstorm together all possible options to solve a situation. The more options you have, the less trapped you'll probably feel. Accept all possible options suggested by your partner regardless if you like them or not. One of you can write them down to keep track of all of them.

3. Together, pick two or three of the most reasonable and fair solutions from the list.

4. List the advantages and disadvantages (pros and cons) of each option. This means that you'll have two or three different lists of advantages or disadvantages.

5. Select together the best option that is apparent from the analysis of advantages and disadvantages.

6. Decide together when and where you will begin to implement the solution that you have selected.

7. After the solution has been implemented, evaluate the outcome of your efforts.

8. Brainstorm together if any changes need to be made in the conflict solution that you selected for it to be even more effective.

Taking the time to go through this exercise can give you an idea of your partner's willingness to work with you in finding solutions, as well as his or her disposition to compromise.

SELF-RESPECT VS. THE RELATIONSHIP

What if an issue is so important to you that it goes against your self-respect? Many times this type of disagreement is related to a strong value you hold for yourself; a lot of people call them *deal breakers (credit where it's due here to Tina Fey, naturally)*. These deal breakers are very disappointing and hurtful, since they can communicate disrespect to you as an individual, or lack of caring from your partner. What are some of your deal breakers? I suggest assessing what situations and issues are deal breakers for you, and that you communicate them to your partner in advance.

If you can obtain the same information from your partner it will help you prepare for the next time the situation comes along, or avoid acting in ways that could create conflict. By communicating these deal breakers to your partner, you're giving him or her a chance to show you that they love and care about you. Listen to your partner's view of your deal breakers to assess your willingness to be flexible, or reflect on why this deal breaker is so important. Maybe it doesn't have to be a deal breaker anymore, but only you can make that decision.

Chapter 9

DEMONSTRATING LOVE

W e all want to feel loved and cared for. At times you may feel that your efforts to demonstrate affection go unnoticed. You're not alone; many couples struggle with displays of love and affection. Most likely, you learned to give love in the way your parents or caregivers gave you love. Since you partner grew up in a different home than you, it's very likely that he or she learned to express love in a different manner. This is an important area for couples, since feeling loved can motivate positive behaviors and willingness to improve a relationship. A simple, yet complete description of the importance of this concept is in *The 5 Love Languages* (Chapman 2010). The theory is based on the concept that expression of love falls into five different categories that each of us can identify with in the way we express love, and the way we want to receive love from others. Usually, the way you express love is the way you expect to receive it—but when you don't receive it in the same way, it can be discouraging and disappointing.

Don and Lori came to therapy because despite the love they had for each other and all the efforts they both placed on showing their love, they were both feeling disappointed and even questioned such love. Don was brought up in a very strict home where he and his siblings were severely punished by their mother if they didn't complete their chores. His father was an alcoholic who at times came home angry and took it out on the family by saying mean things to them. Lori, on the other hand, was brought up in a loving and affectionate home where she felt loved and accepted even after her parents divorced when she was a teenager; her parents still spent a lot of time with her and gave her attention. Don and Lori struggled with their different ways of showing love and affection to each other. They were both stuck on their own way, which got them nowhere. Don and Lori learned the five love languages seen below:

Words of Affirmation
Quality Time
Receiving Gifts
Acts of Service
Physical Touch

Words of affirmation is a form of love expression through words. The use of encouraging and motivating words such as "you can do it!" and "I believe in you!" in times of insecurity are examples of words of affirmation. Another is the use of kind words when your partner makes a mistake (since no one is perfect and your partner may not always do what is best). On the other hand, if you have used harsh words in the past, it's wise to ask for forgiveness in an attempt to repair the damage (see chapter 3 for more on forgiveness). Words are important, so if you use negative, critical or derogatory words, you need to be aware that you're causing deep damage if your partner has this love language—be extra-careful with what you say. Using humble words instead of making demands can make a big difference (See chapter 6). Using positive statements about your partner when you're describing them to others is also part of words of affirmation.

This love language may be difficult, or even feel unnatural to you, but the use of words to affirm love towards your partner may have to be learned in an effort to communicate your love language. Hearing "I love you," or the reasons why you're loved, or simply hearing unsolicited compliments are a must for this language. If you or your partner identify with this love language, you'll benefit from remembering that words are important.

Examples of words of affirmation:

"You look good in that outfit!"
"I love you."
"You're a great _____."

Exercises that you can do to demonstrate your love with words of affirmation:

- You can write a love letter, email or text your partner, since written words can be read over and over again and they can provoke the same positive feelings they did the first time.
- You can also make a commitment to compliment your partner daily.

Quality time is a form of expressing love through spending time with your partner. I'm not talking about sitting on the couch together watching TV while you play with your phone (and I don't mean it simply as a euphemism for sex, either-we're getting there, just one more chapter!). This is about quality, not quantity. Quality time is about togetherness, which means providing focused, undivided attention towards your partner in an effort for him or her to feel loved. Quality conversations are important, since they facilitate sharing of thoughts, feelings, and desires. Active listening is an important aspect of quality time (you can go back to chapter 4 for tips on active listening). Listening to your partner will fulfill their need to feel loved. Spending quality time with the objective of experiencing something together—something you enjoy or that your partner enjoys—creates positive moments for your memories of love for each other.

Exercises that you can do to demonstrate your love with quality time:

- Plan activities together where you can spend one-on-one time, like taking a walk, watching the sunset, etc.
- Ask questions about your partner's past.
- Create a sharing time with your partner where you both have the opportunity to talk.

Receiving gifts is a form of expressing love through gifts. It's about the thoughtfulness and efforts behind giving a gift. An individual whose love language is gifts thinks "She must be thinking about me." The gift is a symbol of that thought of love. If money or finances are an issue, your gift does not have to be expensive—remember, it's the thought behind that gift. Think about the money you spend on a gift as an investment in your relationship. More importantly, if your partner's love language is receiving gifts, the most important gift you could ever give him/her is your presence, especially in a moment of crisis. If your partner says, "I really want you to be here tonight," take that seriously, since the gift of presence is the most powerful gift you can give.

Exercises that you can do to demonstrate your love with gifts:

- Make a gift for your partner.
- Give your partner a gift every day for one week. Think about his or her favorite candy, flowers, or hobby.

Acts of service is a form of expressing love by taking over your partner's responsibilities. This love language can be difficult to learn due to existing stereotypes and possible cultural differences. If you are living in America in the 21st century, many of the stereotypes you grew up with about the roles of men and women no longer apply. In a society where both partners usually have to work, or one partner decides to work at home by raising the children, there are many responsibilities to take care of in the home. If your partner's love language is acts of service, and you're struggling to express this love language, I suggest that you reconsider your beliefs about the roles of men and women in society—otherwise, you may grow to feel resentful of your partner. I also want you to consider that if you choose to act out this love language, you should be doing it from a place of love, not because you're being manipulated to do so. If the latter is the case, I want you to discuss it with your partner. If you cannot reach an understanding, consider therapy as an alternative.

Exercises that you can do to demonstrate your love with acts of service:

- Make a list of all the requests that your partner has made of you over the past weeks. Select one of these each week and do it as an expression of love.
- Be mindful of your partner's requests and remember what they mean for him or her.

- If you have children, recruit their help with some acts of service for your partner.

Physical touch is a form of expressing love through physical affection, such as hugs, kisses, holding hands, and sex. You might lovingly touch your partner almost anywhere in an effort to express love, even though not all touches are equal since some bring more pleasure than others. If touch is your partner's love language, you may benefit from working on this language. Remember that the body is for touching in a loving relationship. If you and your partner are going through a crisis, holding your partner may be all you need to do in that moment to show him or her that you're there.

Exercises that you can do to demonstrate your love with physical touch:

- As you walk together, reach out and hold your partner's hand.
- When you see your partner after a workday, meet him or her with a big hug and kiss.
- Initiate sex.
- Give your partner a massage.

Often I see individuals struggling because they place great effort on trying to show love and affection in the way that they would like to receive it. Your love language is most likely not your partner's love language. If it were, you would have far less trouble in this area. If you do not know your partner's love language and vice versa, it can feel like you're speaking two different languages. Imagine that your partner only speaks Chinese and you only speak English—it would be very difficult to communicate. In the same way, knowing your partner's love language can help you better understand each other.

Remember Don and Lori? Don learned that Lori's love language was quality time. On the other hand, Lori learned that Don's love languages were words of affirmation and acts of service. Once they both had a new understanding in this area, they could concentrate their efforts where they really count. There is no one-way to express love that is "better" than the other, they're just different. By learning what works for you and your partner, you'll be more effective in expressing your love, and asking for what you need from your partner. You can visit http://www.5lovelanguages.com/profile/couples/ to take the 30 questions test that will help you determine your love language. You can also ask your partner to take the test in order to help you show them love in a more effective way, since finding out how your partner understands love can be a key to the success in your relationship.

If your partner's love language is different than yours (which will most likely be the case), you may have to put effort into trying something different that may feel rare or weird to you. You may not be used to your partner's love language, but you need to realize that it's about the quality that your efforts bring to your partner. If this is a problem area, I imagine that you have already been working really hard on trying to show or receive love with little success. Expecting your partner to "know" what your love language is may be unrealistic, especially if she or he has not done so already—and it's even worse if you don't know it yourself. Understanding your love language can help you ask for what you need in the relationship. You may have to explain it and be specific about it. Using the communication techniques from Chapter 6 may be a way to go about it.

There is no shame in not knowing how to express or receive love. Everyone does not grow up in loving and caring homes. If this is the case for you or your partner, it is probably causing distress and difficulties in your relationship. Learning to express and receive love can be a trial-and-error effort. If you or your partner does not know how to give or receive love, the good news is that it can be learned—if necessary, with the aid of therapy.

Chapter 10

SEX

The urge to have sex and reproduce is innate, but the act of sex with another partner can be learned and refined. Many people do not realize that sex is mastered with time and experience, so it can be studied, learned, and practiced. Sadly, the subject of sex can be a taboo even in today's modern world. I work with many individuals from different cultures and with various religious beliefs that struggle to talk about sex, express their needs about sex, and identify the role sex plays in loving relationships. Therefore, some end up with unsatisfactory sex lives in their loving relationships.

Often times I get asked: How often should we be having sex? My answer is: How often are you having sex? And are you satisfied with that? There is no magic number for the frequency of sexual encounters a couple should have; recent studies discovered that individuals seek quality sex over quantity (Muise, Impett, & Desmarais, 2013). Previously, the perceived norm about sex has been linked to how an individual sees his or her own normative group comparing on age, gender, illness status, religiosity, etc. (Donnelly & Burgess, 2008). This means that ideas about how often couples have sexual encounters are determined by perception, as well as social and cultural expectations. Because sex is usually a taboo and families are not talking about it, individuals can learn misleading expectations about sex through movies, TV, peers, and the internet.

SEXUAL SATISFACTION & RELATIONSHIP SATISFACTION

There are different opinions about the role of sexual satisfaction in relationships. Evolutionary Theory argues that the underlying motivation is to reproduce and pass genes from generation to generation (Buss, & Shackelford, 1997). Symbolic Interaction Theory states that sexuality is part of the interaction between the individual and various contexts (LaRossa & Reitzes, 1993), and Script Theory proposes that individuals in sexual relationships adhere to various sexual scripts, the scripts being based on culture and relational levels (Gagnon, 1990). Even though reasons behind the relation between sexuality and relationships satisfaction differ, it has been determined that they can influence one another. Hence, there is a relationship between sexual satisfaction and relationship satisfaction in dating and married couples (Sprecher, 2002; Edwards & Booth, 1994).

In the beginning of a relationship couples usually feel intense sexual desire for one another. If you recall the stages of love in chapter 1, you may remember that *lust* is the craving for sexual gratification, which begins a process that can later evolve into mature love. But what are other factors that lead to sex decreasing over time? Studies have identified other common reasons that sex decreases in long-term relationships:

- *Passage of Time* is related to a slow in sexual activity in a committed relationship (Edwards & Booth, 1994). It's assumed that after an individual starts feeling comfortable and secure in a relationship, sex starts losing the novelty it once had. (Call, Sprecher, & Schwartz, 1995).

- *Stressors in the Relationship* vary according to the stage of the relationship. For example, a common stressor in younger couples is late term pregnancy (De Judicibus & McCabe, 2002), and later breastfeeding and fatigue can also lead to decreases in sexual activity and desire.

- *Time Demands* of daily responsibilities like full-time employment, opposing shifts, raising children, and caring for elderly or ill parents (Donnelly, 1993; Christopher & Sprecher, 2000).

- *Illness or Disabilities*, either one or both partners. Physical illness (e.g. cancer, diabetes, high blood pressure, coronary artery disease and neurological diseases), as well as mental disorders (e.g. anxiety, depression, Post-Traumatic Stress Disorder, sexual abuse) can create temporary or permanent changes in libido (Schmitt & Neubeck, 1985; Wright, Wright, Perry, & Foote-Ardah, 2007).

- *Guilt or Conflict* due to religious beliefs. Being constantly exposed to religious teachings that prohibit sexual practices may lead to repression of sexuality, even within the marriage (Davidson, Darling, Anderson, & Norton, 1995).

Furthermore, a study that assessed individuals in long term relationships and their decision to stay in a marriage where they were involuntarily restrained from sexual activity with their partner (Donnelly & Burgess, 2008) found common factors that lead to this involuntary decrease in sexual activity: lack of interest by partner, relationship problems (like the many that we have discussed and will continue to discuss in this book), concerns with physical appearance, addictions, physical or mental illness, infidelity, pregnancy/childbirth, low sexual desire, and sexual dysfunctions or difficulties. The same study found that individuals in dissatisfied sexual relationships feel frustrated, depressed, rejected, have difficulty concentrating, and experience low self-esteem. The longer time passes between sexual encounters, the more individuals feel despair of ever having a normal sexual relationship, and even hope for the future of the relationship (Donnelly, Burgess, Anderson, Davis, & Dillard, 2001).

After reading about the common factors that lead to decreased sexual activity in couples, as well as the factors that prevent couples from engaging in sexual activity, keep in mind that often two or more of these factors take place at the same time—creating a more complex situation for repair attempts. Surprisingly, some individuals can learn to live with less sex in their long-term committed relationship because they find other payoffs, such as friendship and companionship (Donnelly & Burgess, 2008).

SEXUAL DESIRE

Humans experience unique sexual responses as a result of biological, environmental and cultural mechanisms (Fotopoulou & Fisher, 2012). For centuries, the search for aphrodisiacs to increase sexual desire has continued. From oysters to ginseng roots to various prescription drugs, the list is extensive, but what really creates sexual desire? It has been concluded through scientific studies that the real aphrodisiacs can exist within you (Fisher 2010). These studies also found that in order for sexual desire to develop, the following need to be in place:

- Lust
- Trust
- Love
- Feeling fulfilled in your relationship

What happens when one partner has more sexual desire than the other? First, I would like to start by clarifying that it's completely normal and common for this to happen, given the uniqueness of individuals' experiences mentioned before. Let's take what we have learned so far in this chapter. If there is no lust, trust, or love, and if your relationship is not fulfilling, you'll most likely experience sexual dissatisfaction (as well as relationship dissatisfaction).

Another concept to explore in relation to sexual desire is that desire requires two opposite forces: freedom and commitment (Perel 2006). In other words, if you do not feel free to be yourself and express your inhibited sexual desires, as well as have the freedom to make choices, your desires may be repressed. If a balance between these two forces does not exist, sexual desire may suffer. Additionally, feeling secure and safe in your relationship as a result of your commitment to (and perceived commitment from) your partner can unleash desires of a sexual nature, as mentioned before.

When exploring the frequency and level of satisfactions of sexual activity in your relationships, keep in mind the information that you have learned so far. If you are dissatisfied with your sex life in your committed relationship, the first step that you can take is to communicate this fact to your partner—he or she may not know how you feel. If you're both informed, you can work together at making changes and improvements in your sex life.

USE SEX WISELY

Sex is an important factor in your relationship, but it's also a pleasurable activity. Think about the reasons that you seek sex in your relationship. Sex, like any other pleasurable activity, can become a coping mechanism to avoid negative feelings and stressors, which can lead to sex losing meaning in your relationship, as well as leading to sexual addictions.

Seeking sex with the purpose of increasing intimacy in your relationship is associated with personal and relational benefits, such as a greater sense of well being, enhanced relationship satisfaction, and more positive sexual experiences (Cooper, Barber, Zhaoyang, & Talley, 2011; Impett, Peplau, & Gable, 2005).

Think beyond the act of sex. As mentioned in Chapter 9, sex is a form of physical touch. This means it's a way of expressing connection, affection, and love. Therefore, you can use sex as mean of demonstrating the love that you have for your partner.

WHAT YOU CAN DO TO IMPROVE YOUR SEX LIFE

Assess tension or conflict in your relationship, since it can relate to (and even create a decrease in) sexual activity. Address and work on solving ongoing sources of tension or conflict.

Communicate sexual desires in the moment as much as possible. Even if you are not able to follow through or engage in your sexual desires immediately, it will keep you thinking about them if you talk to your partner about them. He or she will also think about it, and it'll more likely create desire for your partner as well. Sharing your sexual desires with your partner will improve the chances of it actually happening if you're both on board.

Just like it's important to communicate your desires, it's also important to communicate lack of sexual desire, since it can help you explore and assess causes (e.g. physical, emotional, stressors) and find solutions, or look for additional help if needed.

Make time for sex. This means scheduling if necessary. Making time for sex in advance can help you increase the chances that you'll actually engage in sexual activity, because you're making it a priority and creating a space in your busy schedule. Think about all the things that you make time for in your agenda or calendars—why shouldn't sex be one of them? Don't feel that you have to wait for just the right moment, or for the sun to go down, or for things to happen "organically." It may not sound traditionally romantic, but remember how we went over the misconceptions our society and pop culture perpetuates about sex? This is one of those. Pencil in some time, and go for it!

Initiate sex or foreplay with your partner. Do not wait for your partner to approach you, since by doing so, not only are you creating an intimate moment with your partner, but you're also demonstrating he or she is desired. Feeling desired can be exciting and arousing for your partner. Think about how you feel when you're sexually desired.

Making attempts to improve your sex life—just like your relationship—takes work. You may not see immediate changes, but over time you could. Take your time and experiment, because some things may work for you and your partner and others will not... but you won't know unless you try them.

Monica and Sam came into therapy reporting a poor sex life. They were both working professionals raising two small children. Sam expressed his sexual desire for his wife and his feelings of rejection when she turned him down. Monica described her sexual desire as "low," and reported feeling tired after going out to eat at least four times per week with Sam's family which ended in late nights for the entire family. During their time in therapy it was discovered that Monica also had sexual desires for Sam, but she was not as expressive as he was about them. She also felt distanced from him because they spent so much time with his family and their kids, and not enough time as a couple. The couple cut back on dinners out with Sam's family and started scheduling date nights and sex weekly. Sam started to spend more time on foreplay since he learned that Monica needed more than just the act of sex. The couple also made an attempt to spend quality time together after the kids went to bed, which they used to talk about their day, their dreams and aspirations. Monica reported that this time spent together created intimacy, closeness, and a sense of fulfillment in their relationship; ultimately, it increased her sexual desire towards Sam. Monica also learned that sex was a love language (see chapter 10) for Sam and that expressing her sexual desire towards him in the moment was a way to show him love and affection even if it was not possible to act on these desires.

Sam and Monica spent a lot of time avoiding talking about their feelings towards sex and the impact it had on their lives. They carried feelings of disappointment about each other, and it wasn't until they came to therapy that everything was aired out and they could move forward to finding alternative solutions to their situation. Talking about sex in your relationship may be uncomfortable and even scary at times, but avoiding the subject can lead to making many incorrect assumptions about your partner's beliefs and intentions. I strongly encourage you to talk sex with your partner often, since you may learn something interesting, or want to try something new. If you don't discuss it with your partner you may lose an opportunity for shared pleasure and excitement in your life.

Chapter 11

TRUST & BETRAYAL

This entire chapter is dedicated to the importance of trust in a loving relationship. Trust is part of the foundation of a relationship since without it, insecurities, pain, suffering and much disappointment can occur. The Merriam-Webster dictionary defined trust (2014) as the belief that someone or something is reliable, good, honest, effective, etc. Ideally, you would like to believe that your partner is reliable, honest, and that he or she has the best intentions and wishes towards you. Unfortunately, that is not always the case for some relationships.

People have different ideas of how to trust others. For example, you may choose to trust others unless given a reason to distrust, or on the other hand you may be distrustful until given reasons *to* trust. This will heavily depend on your life experiences, the examples you had from your parents, others close to you, and even cultural influences. If you saw your parents or caregivers struggle with trust and lie to each other, it may be understandable that you struggle trusting your partner. If this is the case, and your partner has not given you any legitimate reasons to be distrustful, then conversely he or she may struggle with your difficulty trusting them.

Even if you have no issues with trust in the beginning of your relationship, incidents such as lies and infidelity can corrode the trust you have for your partner, or the other way around. When you have been hurt, it's only natural that your trust is broken. Trust seems to be easy to lose, but difficult to gain back, since that means allowing oneself to be vulnerable and taking the risk of being hurt again. Many couples seek therapy in an attempt to rebuild their trust, since their own efforts usually are not enough to accomplish their objective. In order to build or rebuild trust in your relationship both you and your partner need to be involved, since individual efforts can be discouraged by distrustful behaviors. For example, if you're trying to trust your partner after they lied about their whereabouts, it may be extremely difficult to do so if he or she continues lying.

One major reason that couples struggle with trust issues is past or present betrayals in the relationship. I've seen couples come into therapy after years of difficulty trusting due to betrayals from their past. Betrayal can bring a roller coaster of emotional turmoil into a relationship such as doubts about love, insecurities, vulnerability, anger, disgust, sadness etc. The following are different ways that partners perceive a betrayal of trust (Gottman 2011):

- **Violations of commitment** to being in a relationship. This usually means that your commitment to the relationship is conditional. If you or your partner is waiting for someone "better" to come along, this translates directly to your doubts about the future of your relationship. The conditions can be many things such as illness, financial stability, stress, physical appearance, etc.

- **Betrayal of emotional, romantic or sexual exclusivity.** Aside from the sexual betrayal, intimate, emotional, platonic connections or attachments with others outside the relationship can create feelings of betrayal for partners. Many times, the betrayals of an emotional and romantic nature can be more hurtful than any sexual activity.

- **Secrets, lies, and deception** can be another way to create distrust and a sense of betrayal in your relationship. Think about broken promises, inconsistencies, omitting or hiding information, and pretense towards partners. All of the above are violations of confidence and the trust that has been given.

- **Coalition against your partner** is yet another way to create distrust and betrayal in your relationship. Examples are talking behind your partner's back, or forming an alliance with another person or family member(s) against your partner that hurts or excludes your partner.

- **Betrayal by disinterest** or rejection of your partner's ideas, thoughts, wishes, and interests.

- **Betrayal by unfairness or lack of care.** This is the violation of agreements for fairness involving finances, resources, responsibilities, and time not being shared equally. There is a lack of support and understanding for one another, especially in a moment of need.

- **Betrayal of affection** towards your partner by being cold or unresponsive to emotional needs for fondness.

- **Betrayal by lack of sexual interest.** Demonstrating a lack of attraction, interest, and physical intimacy towards partner.

- **Betrayal by abuse** of any kind. Emotional abuse can be: social isolation, sexual coercion, extreme jealousy, public humiliation, belittling, degradation, threats of violence or other acts that influence fear, damage of property, pets or children. Physical abuse can be categorized as any unwanted touch.

- **Betrayal by disrespect** towards a partner like mockery, sarcasm, ridicule, denigration, and contempt, which asserts superiority instead of complimenting or expressing pride for a partner's accomplishments.

- **Betrayal by not meeting each other's needs**—or at least conscious attempts to meet a partner's essential needs in a relationship (as mentioned before in Chapter 6). Think about emotional availability, openness, and responsiveness towards a partner.

- **Betrayal by breaking sacred promises and vows.** Making promises that are not kept, or making promises that one does not intend to keep.

Eva came into therapy devastated by a recent discovery that her husband of 30 years had been having an affair with a woman he met online. She had suspected that there was something different about her husband for the last couple of months, but he denied any events, his distancing, and irritability towards Eva. He even called her "crazy" when she provided examples of his change in demeanor. One day, Eva's husband was scheduled to go out of town for business as he usually did, but she recalled that there was something different about this day. He left earlier than usual and did not say goodbye. Eva woke up to her husband being gone. She started having a bad feeling throughout the morning, and then remembered that she and her husband had an application on their phones with a GPS in case they ever lost their phones. She opened the phone application to find out that her husband's phone was a couple of blocks away from her business, at a motel. Eva left her office and drove to the motel. She had been waiting for about an hour when she saw her husband coming out of a room with another woman.

Eva was shocked. She described driving home and falling into a rollercoaster of emotions, sadness, anger, hurt, betrayal, and disappointment. Her husband came home earlier than usual and to his surprise Eva was home (which wouldn't normally happen). Eva described confronting her husband, who continued denying the situation until Eva explained that she had seen him. At that point, he finally admitted that he had been having an affair with another woman whom he met online, who traveled from California to Florida to meet him. Eva expressed the pain she felt when her husband told her that he was confused and didn't know if he wanted to be with her.

Betrayal is often times an impactful and traumatic event in the life of any individual. In Eva's case, she went on to feel irritability, aggression, numbness (after the discovery of betrayal), obsession, and shifting emotions, all of which have been identified as common traumatic reactions (Glass 2004). The severity of the traumatic reaction is determined by the following factors, which interact with one another in establishing the intensity, scope, and persistence of the traumatic reaction:

1. How the discovery was made. Was it a confession? Was there an informant? Was it an accidental discovery?
2. The extent of shattered assumptions: about the relationship (e.g. "I never doubted that we loved each other"), the partner (e.g. "I thought you would always be honest"), and self (e.g. "I knew I was getting old and unattractive").
3. Individual vulnerabilities (e.g. low self-esteem) and situational vulnerabilities (e.g. family history of betrayal, couple's history of betrayal, past trauma, etc.)

4. The nature of the betrayal, such as the extent of the damage caused by the betrayal and the duration of betrayal.

5. Whether the threat of the betrayal continues.

In my work with couples I see time after time how difficult it can be for a partner who has engaged in behaviors that caused betrayal to accept and take responsibility for the damage that has been done. Common reactions of the betrayer have also been identified (Glass 2004) as: resentment, impatience, and grief about hurting a partner or ending an affair. This makes it difficult for the betraying partner to engage with / help the other partner heal.

The first step is for the betrayed partner to decide to rebuild a new relationship— otherwise it can be extremely difficult to get through the day-to-day struggles of rebuilding trust. This may bring a lot of ambivalence and mixed feelings on the part of both partners. The following is a proposal by John Gottman (2011) to heal from betrayal step by step:

Phase 1: Partners express remorse, establish transparency, and create understanding, acceptance, and the beginnings of forgiveness. This first phase is concentrated mainly in the betrayed partner.

1. **The Betrayer listens to repeated expressions of hurt feelings by the betrayed partner without defensiveness** (this step is easier said than done). When I treat couples that struggle with betrayal, I find that the betrayer has a difficult time listening and not being defensive. This reaction can be the result of feeling guilty, fear to further hurt the partner, the desire to feel understood, the need to be rational or logical about his or her actions, or the partner simply may not be ready to take responsibility for the pain caused. I have seen individuals

struggle to take this step and as a result, jeopardize their chances to rebuild trust and a new relationship.

2. **The betrayer expresses genuine remorse** for the pain caused. Otherwise, it will be extremely difficult for the betrayed partner to risk trusting again. This step usually entails questions and answers about the betrayal, with the purpose of creating transparency and honesty in regard to it. It is said that this step can begin to reverse the post-traumatic stress reaction caused by the betrayal.

3. **Creating transparency, verification, and the "don't rock the boat" rule.** The transparency is necessary in an effort to demonstrate that your partner can be relied upon, since it's usually the case the hurt or betrayed individual feels like he or she no longer knows the betrayer. The "don't rock the boat" rule means that both individuals do not want to destroy the fragile state of rebuilding trust, so they offer cooperation, reassurance, respect, and avoid frightening the betrayed partner. The betrayed partner cooperates too, as long as there is mutual cooperation.

4. **Creating understanding by individualizing the "process of betrayal."** This is about gaining an understanding of the conditions that led to the betrayal, by identifying negative patterns in the couple's history that led the relationship to become vulnerable. Changes in behavior must occur on the part of the betrayer in order to demonstrate remorse at this point.

5. **Processing major emotional wounds.** The couple needs to learn factors that trigger conflict avoidance, turning away, conflict escalation and anger in an effort to accept vulnerabilities. They also need to understand the meaning behind the betrayer's decision to work on the relationship and stay with the hurt partner.

6. **Establishing a process for maximizing cooperation.** This fragile process consists of one partner choosing to cooperate in an effort to have the other partner follow the example, unless there is new evidence of potential betrayal and distrust by the betrayer.

7. **The hurt partner accepts apology, and begins to forgive.** In order for this step to take place, the hurt partner needs to keep seeing genuine remorse via behavioral change towards transparency. The hurt partner chooses to begin forgiving by demonstrating a continuing willingness to cooperate, even in the face of uncertainty and possible mistakes. This step can take much time to complete, given the depth of the hurt.

Phase 2: Reversing betrayal processes that have been active in the relationship. After beginning the process to forgive, this second stage of rebuilding trust is about identifying vulnerabilities and addressing these vulnerabilities.

1. **Learning constructive conflict and self-disclosure, as opposed to conflict avoidance or escalation.** After distrust, a tendency to avoid conflict or become absorbed by the conflict takes prevalence. It's important that couples learn to disclose and express their needs, even when it is most difficult. As mentioned earlier, it's important to be able to express feelings and needs so you can give your partner a better opportunity to fulfill them.

2. **Agreeing to the principle of mutually meeting needs.** This step is important since it provides an opportunity to demonstrate loyalty, and priority of the relationship by committing to make an attempt to meet your partner's needs.

3. **Agreeing to turn toward bids in sliding-door moments.** Gottman refers to *bids in sliding-door moments* as the

opportunity to connect with your partner when he or she needs your attention, instead of turning away and eroding trust over time. It's about everyday moments when you can choose to ignore your partner or hope that he or she provides love, acknowledgement, shares laughter, kisses or hugs, even an "I love you." I encourage you to pay attention to how often you turn away from your partner when he or she needs your attention. If you notice that you do, make a conscious effort to respond in a loving manner.

4. **The couple creates a lasting behavior change of cherishing as opposed to trashing.** The betrayer expresses genuine and strong intentions to change their behavior and engage in patterns of thinking that promote strength in the relationship. Cherishing your partner needs to become an essential part of your relationship.

5. **The couple establishes norms that are set up in order to "create the sacred" in the relationship.** Creating a new set of rules for the relationship requires personal sacrifice. The creation of new rules symbolizes the creation of a new relationship. Part of solidifying these rules is to communicate to others involved with your relationship about the new rules.

Phase 3: Building Trust and Intimate Trust.

1. **Learning the skills of intimate conversation.** Expressing emotions, probing, following up, exploration, and empathy are skills that lead to intimate conversations. Sharing goals and dreams are also intimate conversations. Try to have intimate conversations daily in an effort to promote trust and intimacy.

2. **Increasing mutual dependency in the relationship.** This means actively engaging in investment, sacrifice, and pro-

relationship thinking--which all lead to commitment to your relationship.

3. **Set up a high cost for subsequent betrayal.** There needs to be an understanding that subsequent untrustworthiness will have severe consequences for the relationship. This is not a threat, but the result of actions and consequences, which can be a motivating force for individuals to keep focused on their choice to commit to their relationship.

4. **Create personal sex and intimate trust.** This process begins with knowledge about each other's personal preferences in sex, love and romance, as part of building emotional connection. Talk to your partner about his or her preferences, since ignorance often leads to mistaken assumptions.

Remember that all of this hard work will be disregarded if distrustful behaviors continue to be present in the relationship. More so, these phases and steps can be extremely difficult to implement and act on, given the emotional roller coaster that comes with betrayal for both partners. Seeking professional help to recover from betrayal is highly recommended, given the difficulty of the recovery, the length of the process, and the emotionality that comes with it.

INFIDELITY

If you have experienced infidelity, either on your part or your partner's, you may benefit from reading the remainder of this chapter. If this is not the case, you're welcome to skip this section and continue to the following chapter on the importance of friendship in a loving relationship. Infidelity is a major cause for distrust and betrayal in many relationships. Perhaps unsurprisingly, sexual infidelity has been identified as the primary cause for divorce (Amato & Rogers 1997).

In working with couples that struggle with the aftereffects of infidelities, I have noticed the abundance of myths about love and infidelity that exist out there. I would like to share the following facts about love and infidelity that may help you reflect on your outlook.

Facts you need to know about love with infidelity (Glass 2004):

- People compare and confuse the intensity of being "in love" during an affair with the secure, comfortable feeling of reality-based "loving" that occurs in long-term relationships.
- The feeling of being "in love" is linked to passion and infatuation.
- True love, which people grow into, is characterized by acceptance, understanding, and compassion. That is why so few people end up marrying their affair partner, and those who do have an extremely high probability of divorce.
- Once the affair is no longer the forbidden relationship that takes place in a golden bubble, the cold light of day soon bursts the romantic fantasies.
- A happy marriage is not a vaccine against infidelity.
- The person having the affair may not be giving enough at home, rather than getting enough.
- It is normal to be attracted to another person, but fantasizing about what it would be like to be with that person is a danger sign.
- Flirting is crossing the line, because it is an invitation that indicates receptivity.
- Infidelity is not about love or sex. It's about maintaining appropriate boundaries with others and being open and honest in your committed relationship.
- You do not have to have sexual intercourse to be unfaithful. Passionate kissing or oral sex is a violation of your commitment to your partner.

- Emotional affairs are characterized by secrecy, emotional intimacy, and sexual chemistry. An emotional affair can be more threatening to a relationship than brief sexual flings.

It's important to first clarify that in the case of betrayal due to an infidelity, both partners have to decide to rebuild a new relationship. Secondly, the other relationship needs to end in order to make an attempt to rebuild trust. If the other relationship is not over, it will be almost impossible for couples to build trust. A third person will distract the betrayer from placing needed efforts into rebuilding the relationship, since loyalty can become divided between the partner and the third person.

Qualities that can help an unfaithful partner regain trust, minimize the damage, and move forward towards reparation have been identified (MacDonald 2010) as:

- Understanding the wrongness of their behaviors.
- Understanding the depth of the pain they've caused.
- Resiliency to withstand all the emotional ups and downs once the truth comes to light.
- Realistic expectations about the time it takes to rebuild trust, and the scars that will remain.
- Demonstrate respect for the betrayed partner's choices on how to proceed after the betrayal.

These qualities are easier said than done, given all of the emotions involved, so how do you translate these into action? You can start with the following useful tips (MacDonald 2010):

- Tell the truth, rather than waiting to be discovered. This first step can help you avoid more doubts from your partner in the course of recovery. This will increase the chances that the relationship will survive. I have heard time after time "all I ever wanted was for him/her to be honest." Telling the truth can show your partner that you're ready to start being honest, which ultimately will help start to rebuild the trust.

- If the affair comes to light through discovery instead of disclosure, show instant remorse, and try your best to avoid defensiveness. Instant sadness and remorse are humbling. Many times attitudes and justifications get in the way of sincere remorse. Helpful statements:
    o "I was wrong."
    o "I deeply regret hurting you this way."
    o "If I could do things over, I never would have become involved with _____."

- Willingly breaking off all contact with the affair partner, including phone calls, texting, emails, and physical presence. Refusal to break contact will be perceived by your partner as you choosing your affair partner over them--not something that will help create trust. Two former patients of mine, Heidi and Oliver, came to therapy after Oliver discovered that Heidi was having an affair. Heidi's refusal to break contact with her affair partner continued to erode the trust that both she and Oliver wanted to rebuild. Ultimately, Oliver filed for divorce.

- Allow your spouse to determine if, how, and when any final "closure" is allowed between you and your affair partner. Effective disclosures usually include:
    o A declaration of love for the spouse.
    o An admission that the relationship was wrong.
    o A firm insistence that the relationship is over.
    o A request for the affair partner to make no further contact with you or other family members.

- Including your partner in this process will be perceived by them as willingness to cooperate, consideration of their feelings, and respect.

- No more lies or hiding information. No more secrets. Lies and secrets eventually come to light, and continuing them after the affair has been discovered will only hurt your partner (contrary to the belief of many to protect them from more suffering). Tamara said to me during one of our sessions "I kept giving him a chance to come clean, but the continued lying only made it worse."

- Accept full responsibility for the decision to have an affair. Explore the reasons for your predisposition to affairs by seeking professional help. Despite the factors that made your relationship vulnerable for an affair, you had a choice, and maybe you went with the poor choice of pursuing the affair, but it was still a choice. No one forced you. In addition, taking responsibility is a form of effective communication and can lead to emotional closeness during conflict.

- Have patience with your hurt partner and the time needed to recover. Avoid statements like:
  - "Why can't you move on?"
  - "You should be over this by now!"
  - "What's your problem? I said I was sorry!"
  - "Don't you think you're overreacting?"
  - "Well, you did ____ to me."
  - "You're just bitter and vindictive."
  - "You've hurt me too!"
  - "Why can't you just forgive and forget?"
  - If patience is not your strength, this can be challenging, but do your best since patience communicates caring.

- Seek to understand your partner's pain. If you have a hard time understanding your partner's feelings, try giving your partner room to vent and grieve in your presence. Here is where you'll need to apply the patience that was mentioned before.
- Be aware of your partner's pain. Avoid allowing self-pity to distract you. This is a situation where being able to talk to a professional can help you release your feelings of guilt and regret in a safe environment, without sabotaging your efforts to rebuild your relationship.
- Learn to increase your abilities to show sincere empathy and offer heartfelt apologies. Read Chapter 5 of this book to help you with demonstrating empathy and validation towards your partner. Helpful Apologies:
    - "I feel terrible for how badly I've hurt you."
    - "I don't blame you for feeling that way."
    - "I am so sorry for what I did to you."
    - "You didn't deserve that."
    - "I deeply regret hurting you."
    - "That must feel terrible."
    - "I was so wrong."
    - "I will do whatever it takes to make this up to you."
    - "I love you and promise to never betray you again."
- Be sensitive to your partner's distrust and show willingness to do whatever it takes to rebuild that trust. It's absolutely normal for you partner to distrust your actions or intentions, and expecting your partner to do the opposite is unrealistic. Karen expressed her frustration with her husband's difficulty trusting her after her affair. Her husband's response during session was "how can you expect me to trust you? It's not a switch that I turn on and off."

- Respect sensitivities and "triggers" of the affair for your hurt partner. Be aware that anything associated with the affair will be a source of pain to your partner. Allow him or her to choose what to do about these reminders. Comedian Chris Rock has a famous routine where a betrayed wife vents to her husband: "Did you turn left when you were with that b*tch? From now on, no matter where we're going, it's ALL right turns, you hear me?" Of course Rock is exaggerating, but the point is a real one—even seemingly innocuous actions can act as triggers.

- Assume that your partner is continuously tormented by the hurt, memories, and imagined encounters between you and your affair partner. Be proactive about checking in on your partner's emotional status. Keep in mind anticipation and awareness to these incidents, since it will show your caring and respecting of your partner's feelings. Norma was afraid to run into her husband's affair partner at his company's holiday party. Because Norma's husband Felix was aware of her fear he was able stay by Norma's side and demonstrate physical affection, which helped Norma feel more comfortable at the party, but ultimately loved and cared for by Felix.

- If you have children (regardless of their age), recognize the impact and damage of parental affairs upon your children and seek to make amends.

After reading this list, you'll have an idea of the complexity of recovering from an infidelity and betrayal in your relationship. Once again, I would like to emphasize the importance of seeking professional help for your relationship or at a minimum individually, given the depth of the emotional wounds resulting from affairs.

Finally, I would also like to share some statistics about infidelities that may help you get a better idea of the reality of affairs in our culture:

- 40% of women and 60% of men will have an affair at some point or another during their relationship (Vaughan 2003).
- Between 44-55% of married women and 50-60% of married men engage in extramarital sex at some point or another during their relationship (Atwood & Schwartz, 2002).
- 17% of divorces in the United States are caused by infidelity. (www.menstuff.org)
- Only about 3% of a study of successful men surveyed eventually married their affair partners (Halper, 1988).
- Only about 11% of affairs lead to an actual relationship between the betrayer and the affair partner (www.menstuff.org).
- 75% of marriages that begin as affairs fail, partly due to their guilt-filled and untrusting foundations (Staheli, 1998)
- Affairs affect one of every 2.7 couples, according to Janis Abrahms Spring, author of "After the Affair," as reported by the Washington Post (Gerhardt, 1999).
- Evidence supports that there is a correlation between online infidelity and subsequent real-time sexual affairs (www.menstuff.org).
- 10% of extramarital affairs last one day (Lightfoot, 2013).
- 10% last more than one day, but less than a month (Lightfoot, 2013).
- 50% last more than a month but less than a year (Lightfoot, 2013).
- 40% last two or more years. Few extramarital affairs last more than four years (Lightfoot, 2013).
- The average length of an affair is 2 years (www.infidelityfacts.com).
- 31% of marriages last after an affair has been admitted to or discovered (www.infidelityfacts.com).

- 24% of betrayed husbands and wives who knew about their partners' infidelity are severely anxious to the point of panic (Glass & Staeheli, 2004)
- 30% of betrayed partners are clinically depressed (Glass & Staeheli, 2004)

Chapter 12
FRIENDSHIP

B eing friends with your partner is an important aspect of your relationship that leads to increased trust, consideration, and loyalty. Of course, friendship can change with time and painful situations, but it's important to work on maintaining it, since research indicates that friendship affects the way people behave and feel when they disagree (Gottman 1999). The research also suggests that couples with a strong friendship have a lot more access to their humor, affection, and the positive energy that makes it possible to have disagreements or to live with disagreements in a much more constructive and creative way. The conclusion is that the friendship components of the relationship are fundamental for accessing positive emotions during times of disagreement. Three aspects of friendship have been described within relationships (Gottman 1999):

Building Love Maps. Gottman refers to love maps as the roadmap you can create in your mind of your partner's inner psychological world. He describes this ability as the most basic level of friendship. It's about feeling known in the relationship, like your partner is interested in knowing you, and vice versa. Think about what your partner's worries and stresses are at this moment. What are your partner's hopes and aspirations? What are some of his or her dreams, values, and goals? Do you know? If the answer is yes, you're already working on cultivating a friendship with your partner. On the contrary, if the answer is "I'm not sure," or "I don't know", you may benefit from working on this aspect of your relationship, since it creates emotional intimacy and promotes trust. It's important to **ask questions constantly and remember the answers** to those questions. Things change, so **keeping up with asking questions** will help you continuously know about your partner's changes. Keep in mind the need to ask open-ended questions (questions with potentially more than one word answers).

Sharing fondness and admiration is about building affection and respect in the relationship. Gottman explains that there are two parts to nurturing fondness and admiration. First is **creating a mental habit of observing things to admire about your partner, to be proud of and appreciate**. Note that this habit of observing admiration is the opposite of a critical habit where you may be observing your partner's mistakes, or what is he or she is not doing. Second, after observation, the appreciation or admiration needs to be expressed verbally or nonverbally in order for your partner to know about it (it cannot stay hidden). The objective is to point out what your partner is doing right or correctly in your eyes, which leads to a sense of appreciation and respect. Example: "Thank you for doing that. I really appreciate it."

Turning Toward (rather than away). This step is about emotional connection. If you're spending time with your partner you may be sharing your needs verbally or nonverbally. Gottman calls these *"bids"* for emotional connection. Bids are the same as the love languages discussed in Chapter 9. You may be asking for attention, interest, conversation, humor, affection, warmth, empathy, assistance, support, and so on. Gottman explains that these tiny moments of emotional connection form an emotional bank account that gets built over time.

For instance, if you partner says: "I want to learn to play tennis." You could respond, "You always say that you want to do things, but you never do," but this would be turning away from emotional connection. If you instead said "Huh, that could be fun!" you would be showing some acknowledgement and turning towards emotional connection. An even more enthusiastic response to turn toward emotional connection would be "You would be great at tennis, we could play together." Remember, the point is to build an emotional bank account with demonstrations of love and affection that will help you later, especially when you have an argument or a disagreement. The fundamental process of turning toward involves increasing your awareness and mindfulness about how your partner asks for what he or she needs from you (love languages), and seeing the longing behind it that may be a bit negative or unclear. Gottman's study found that couples who were divorced 6 years after their wedding turned towards each other only 33% of the time; the ones still together after 6 years had an 86% turning toward rate. The study also showed that turning toward was related to more affection and humor during conflict.

RESPECT

Building mutual respect is another aspect of friendship with your partner. I mentioned earlier how fondness and admiration promote respect, so keep that in mind as you continue reading. Respect can mean something slightly different for individuals of different cultures, and even within your own culture—given that individuals have different values and beliefs that influence their view of respect. It can be challenging for some to respect different beliefs or values when they do not make logical sense. However, you can learn to respect other's beliefs even if you do not understand or do not agree with the different values. Learning to respect differences can be a helpful tool that you can use during arguments and disagreements with your partner, since many times arguments take place in relation to these differences in opinions (or an inability to accept the differences).

Often times I see individuals in relationships that are constantly disrespecting each other by calling each other names, belittling, being condescending, disregarding requests, and so on. Many times with these disrespecting couples there is a sense of demand for respect. Respect has to be given in order to be received. If you expect your partner to respect you, but you're not acting in a respectful manner, it may never happen. Here are some ways that you can show respect towards your partner (www.twofous.org):

Choose your words carefully. Words cannot be taken back, so being careful and mindful of what comes out of your mouth is important. Insulting or name-calling will most likely promote more aggression (see Chapter 4 on Communication) or fear. Think about the objective you want to accomplish as a result of the conversation, and try to be diplomatic towards your partner. You're probably already being diplomatic and choosing your words carefully at work, so why can't you try to do the same with your partner?

Acknowledging your partner's contributions. Just like fondness and admiration, pointing out what your partner is doing right by acknowledging his or her positive acts towards the relationship can help lower defensive stands, and lead to more respectful and constructive interactions between you and your partner.

Honoring your partner's boundaries. Boundaries are limits that define acceptable behavior; they're unofficial rules about what should be off-limits (http://www.merriam-webster.com) in a relationship. Understanding and respecting your partner's boundaries regarding personal space, time spent together or apart, and physical contact that he or she needs is conducive to demonstrating respect.

Being willing to compromise shows respect because you can place your own priorities or desires aside for the betterment of the relationship; thereby making a statement that your partner and the relationship are a priority to you. Compromising provides needed flexibility to your relationship. Otherwise, every disagreement would be a battlefield.

Showing consideration towards your partner's everyday responsibilities (such as working late or housework) is another way to indicate respect. You can practice showing consideration by being thoughtful and pointing out your partner's efforts to keep the house clean, work in the yard, work to make ends meet, etc.

Be strong enough to admit when you're wrong. If you're confident of your self-worth, then apologizing doesn't have to be a threat to you. Remember that we all make mistakes at some point or another, and no one is perfect. Apologizing when you're wrong will only enhance respect for one another and the love you have for each other. On the other hand, if you apologize too much, it may be a sign of low self worth and insecurities. If the latter is the case, you can work on improving your self-esteem in order to have a more balanced relationship.

Protect your partner's well being physically and emotionally from others—or even yourself. If you struggle with controlling your temper, you may consider seeking professional help to learn more effective ways to cope with intense angry feelings.

If you practice some of these suggestions, you may surprisingly discover that your partner can act in the same way towards you; remember the Golden Rule: treat others how you want to be treated. If this is not the case, and you don't feel respected by your partner, I want you to assess yourself and be mindful in the following areas:

Are you setting and upholding your own boundaries?
Are you acting with integrity?
Are you keeping your word?
Are you showing respect towards your partner?
Do you feel worthy of respect?
Do you believe that you're being physically or emotionally abused?

If the answer to any of these questions is YES, talk to someone you can safely confide in or consider seeking the help of a professional, especially if you're being abused.

POSITIVE MOMENTS (HAVING FUN)

Another aspect of building a friendship with your partner is to have fun together, just like in the beginning of your relationship when you used to laugh together, go places together, and share special moments— all of which helped build a foundation of positive experiences in your relationship. As the years go by, arguments and disagreements can become prevalent in your present relationship. You may have noticed that you and your partner are not having much fun these days, since there is much tension in your interactions. I want you to know that you do not have to wait until things get better in your relationship to create positive moments, since that may take a while. I suggest that you start right away. Here are some ideas that you can try to build positive moments in your relationship, despite your arguments and disagreements.

DATE NIGHT

Scheduling time to spend with your partner (no kids, extended family, or friends) can help create positive interactions between you two. Date nights do not have to be costly. It can be something simple like watching the sunset together, having a picnic at the park, taking a walk with beautiful scenery, etc. Date "night" does not have to be at night either—it can be in the morning or afternoon. As long as you can fit it in your busy schedule, anything counts. The purpose of dates is to spend time together where you can give each other undivided attention. You may consider turning cell phones off or on silent to avoid distractions. One thing that date night is not is watching TV at home. If you're watching TV or a movie, you're not giving each other undivided attention.

APPRECIATION TIME

Take some time daily to let your partner know how much you appreciate him or her, something about them, or what they do. Showing appreciation not only recognizes your partner's positive qualities or attributes, but also keeps those qualities and attributes fresh in your mind, and helps to avoid taking them for granted. I usually suggest scheduling five minutes of daily appreciation time, when you and your partner can share what you appreciate about each other. If you're recognizing what your partner is doing right, there is an increased likelihood that it will happen again.

VACATIONS

Taking time off and away from routine and responsibilities can have a definite impact in building positive memories together. Vacation time is not just about taking an expensive trip out of town or abroad; it can also be taking a day off from responsibilities to spend it with your partner, where you can explore a new neighborhood or sight in your city or town. It can be sharing a new experience together whether it's one mile from your home or 1,000 miles away. Just like date nights, vacations do not have to be an expensive or costly experience. Get creative with your surrounding environment. There is a morning show here in Tampa, Florida called *One Tank Trips*, where the host travels a determined distance finding new and exciting destinations all by using only one tank of gas. Of course you may not live in Florida where the weather facilitates outings, but I can guarantee that wherever you live, there are plenty of sights that you have not visited or explored with your partner.

Morgan and Robert both had jobs that required traveling a couple of times per month. They also had two children and were focused on being involved parents despite their traveling. They were great at being parents and covering for each other while the other was away on business, but their friendship had suffered as a result of their limited time together as a couple. It can be easy to get caught up in routines and taking care of business day after day. Morgan and Robert came to therapy because their friendship was dying and their excitement and admiration for each other were dying with it. After implementing date nights, a couple of romantic getaways, and appreciation time, their friendship started to blossom once again due to the increase in positive moments. Morgan described it as "I forgot how much I liked him. I missed our talks and time together so much that I was resenting him for not trying." By focusing on rebuilding their friendship Morgan and Robert were able to improve other areas of their relationship, such as communication and sex, which had been suffering as a result.

I hope that after reading this chapter, you can identify areas of improvement to promote a deep friendship in your relationship. Since this friendship will serve you in times of conflict and disagreement, it will also create loyalty and trust for each other. Your friendship will help you balance the negative interactions you and your partner have with positive moments built in your memory. Remember, all couples have difficulties and disagreements, but if you have a strong friendship, it can be easier to get through these difficult times together.

Chapter 13

FACTORS THAT IMPEDE PROGRESS OR SUCCESS

D o all relationships have to work out? I'm often faced with this question in one form or another in my work with couples. As a couple's therapist, I would like to be able to help every couple that comes to me asking for help. The truth is that it's not always possible. Many factors can contribute to a relationship ending. In this book, I have tried to address many of the following issues from a different perspective and give you information, as well as some tips and tools to help you work towards improving your relationship. If after reading this or other books on the subject you're still struggling to act on the suggestions given, you should consider seeking the help of a professional that can help you move forward in your relationship. Here are some common reasons relationships do not work out:

1. Not being fully invested into the relationship.
2. Difficulty trusting.

3. Inability to forgive the other for the mistakes made in the past.
4. Abuse, either physical or psychological/emotional.
5. Unrealistic expectations, which usually leads to focusing on the negative.
6. Failure to communicate needs in the relationship.
7. Lack of respect for each other.
8. Inability to reach compromises due to opposite ideals, opinions, or beliefs.
9. Difficulty dedicating time to the relationship.
10. Believing that one **needs** a partner instead of wanting to be with a partner.
11. The existence of an addiction or a mental illness without treatment.

It is important to mention that each one of these areas needs to be addressed separately. If a couple seeks therapy in an effort to improve their relationship and work on any one (or more) of these areas, they will probably have better outcomes in overcoming these difficulties than if they try to solve them by themselves. Many times one or both partners may find it difficult to deal with these issues and decide to end the relationship. Let's examine each of these factors more closely.

NOT BEING FULLY INVESTED IN THE RELATIONSHIP

This is a common situation where much disappointment is created for the partner who is invested in the relationship. Many times, this type of situation creates a sense of unfairness for one or both partners, where there is no balance. Usually, one person feels that he or she is doing more for the other person. Often, this situation arrives due to one or both partners not being fully committed to the relationship.

Many couples don't make it as far as getting married, or if they married young, they struggle with different life goals. Being committed to your relationship is going to be a key element for your relationship to last, since you will face bumpy roads ahead. I've noticed that in my work, when couples have made a decision for themselves and with each other that they will do whatever it takes to save their relationship or marriage, there is a sense of duty that will help them get through the difficulties ahead. I like to use the common phrase "for better or for worse" which is part of the vows that people take when they get married. Many underestimate the "for worse" part of the vows. These will be the challenging parts of your relationship, the times that will make it stronger or break it. Ask yourself the question: Am I fully invested in my relationship? Do I believe my partner is right for me? Are we a good match? If the answer is no, maybe you can explore the roots of your answers and evaluate the reasoning behind it. Your partner most likely already suspects that you're not fully committed.

DIFFICULTY TRUSTING

This is surely one of the most difficult cases to work when helping a couple. It usually requires a lengthy therapy treatment. Whether the trust was broken years before or recently, it's about the impactful or traumatic effect that it had on the individual. Go back to Chapter 11 for common reasons people lose trust in relationships. Many times individuals do not realize that rebuilding trust is a job for two people. It requires both partners to be fully engaged in the process. When one person in the relationship breaks the trust, the hurt partner may not be willing to work to help rebuild the trust. The response that I usually hear in these cases is "this is his or her fault," and the next statement typically something like "why should I have to do anything?"

After explaining the need for the hurt partner to participate in the work, he or she may say "I'll do it IF he or she shows me first." Even though this is a common reaction of self-defense, it gets in the way of the process because it creates a conditional state that may decrease motivation or increase resistance for the other partner. It's my belief that attempts to create trust are better done with the help of a professional, given the difficult nature of the process.

INABILITY TO FORGIVE THE OTHER FOR THE MISTAKES MADE IN THE PAST

If you read Chapter 3 on forgiveness, you may remember that forgiveness is a process, but more so a personal choice to move on from pain. At times there may be so many incidents in the story of a relationship that forgiveness can be a challenging quest, since your innate defense mechanisms or your ego can make it difficult to take the risk to be hurt again. If you or your partner is having difficulty going through the process of forgiveness, you could seek therapy or spiritual counseling for additional assistance. Otherwise, it would make it very difficult for the partner who may be trying to rebuild a relationship to motivate himself/herself to continue making efforts.

ABUSE (PHYSICAL, PSYCHOLOGICAL OR EMOTIONAL)

If you have ever felt abused in a relationship, you may have noticed the fear that comes with thoughts of ending the relationship, no matter how bad things are. If you're in a threatening situation where you feel that your well-being is at risk due to physical or emotional abuse, the safest decision you can make for you and your children (if you have any) is to remove yourself from that situation. My personal belief is that people can change (meaning the abuser), but only if they want to change. However, even if they truly want to change it takes an undetermined amount of time. I do not believe that you or anyone should put their own well-being at risk. If your partner is abusive and he or she wants to change, unless they are taking serious, concrete steps to make it happen (such as seeking professional help), you don't have to wait around. Seek help immediately.

UNREALISTIC EXPECTATIONS

They usually lead to focus on the negative. If you read Chapter 6, you may have a better idea of what expectations are, and how they can affect your relationship. Unrealistic expectations are a very common issue for couples, especially if one or both individuals have not had positive examples about expectations in their lives. Usually, unrealistic expectations can be lowered when another opinion from a respected individual (family member, friend, pastor or bishop, therapist) is presented. However, it may take some time, or require continuous talks about it. If you or your partner have unrealistic expectations about yourself, your partner or relationship, it may be helpful to talk to someone you can trust about it. There also needs to be a willingness to improve as an individual and as a partner. Otherwise, there is no motivation to make things different.

FAILURE TO COMMUNICATE NEEDS IN THE RELATIONSHIP

Chapter 6 addresses the importance of communicating needs. However, there may be underlying difficulties you could encounter in your efforts to communicate these needs. Many times, when individuals have a hard time asking for their needs to be met, it may be related to low self-esteem and self-worth, irrational beliefs about self and others, growing up in a home with a parent who had an addiction or mental illness, and more. Finding the root of your difficulty and learning ways to assert yourself and your needs can be possible.

LACK OF RESPECT FOR EACH OTHER

In Chapter 12 we covered respect as part of the friendship in a relationship. A lack of respect, or a situation where you or your partner cannot demonstrate respect and are constantly engaging in belittling behaviors, condescending comments, contempt, and more, can make it difficult to find solutions, compromises, forgiveness, and communication. If you cannot find respect for your partner, your relationship may be struggle and become vulnerable to negative influences. However, you can learn to respect your partner despite your beliefs. Talk to someone you trust, who can help you move to a more constructive place of respect towards your partner.

INABILITY TO REACH COMPROMISES DUE TO OPPOSING IDEALS, OPINIONS, OR BELIEFS

This is a very common difficulty in relationships. Reaching compromises can be challenging due to strong opinions and deeply rooted beliefs. However, if you can respect your partner and his or her differences it can be easier to achieve compromises (see Chapter 8). Learning to be empathetic and validating (see Chapter 5) towards your partner's feelings and beliefs can help you reach compromises.

DIFFICULTY DEDICATING TIME TO THE RELATIONSHIP

As mentioned in Chapter 12, creating positive memories in your relationship is an important part of your life together. If you are both having a hard time dedicating time to your relationship, your love connection may suffer, and you may not be able to create the positive memories that I mentioned before. More so, it can send the message that your partner is not as important as OTHER things you're occupying your time with. If you're both having difficulty dedicating time to your relationship due to obligations and responsibilities, a need to find some balance will benefit the relationship. If both of you have tried everything in your power to dedicate more time and remain unsuccessful, there may be other underlying issues affecting your ability to do so.

BELIEVING THAT ONE *NEEDS* A PARTNER INSTEAD OF WANTING TO BE WITH A PARTNER

In Chapter 2, I covered the different types of relational attachments and their consequences in relationships. Anxious-Preoccupied and Fearful-Avoidant attachment patterns may struggle with belief of needing a partner versus wanting a partner. Both types of attachment patterns struggle with insecurities about self and acceptance by others. This belief brings a lot of negative feelings for both the individual struggling with them and the partner receiving the impact of them.

THE EXISTENCE OF AN ADDICTION OR A MENTAL ILLNESS WITHOUT TREATMENT

This would apply to one or both individuals in the relationship. Addictions and mental illness come with symptoms and behaviors that can make it extremely difficult to have a relationship. This can be equally difficult for both individuals in the relationship—the one that is struggling with the symptoms and the other who could be affected by them. Marchand and Hock (2000) explained that individual distress has a negative impact on relationship satisfaction regardless of the time the symptoms began. It has also been determined that spouses who were both presenting mental health disorders are among the most difficult to treat in psychotherapy (Whisman, 2001). Here is a list of common mental disorders and how they affect relationships:

Anxiety disorders (General Anxiety Disorder, agoraphobia, specific phobias, OCD, panic disorders) can create more conflict between couples by increasing tension and arguments, restricting activities, and decreasing the attention paid to the needs of the non-anxious partner and instead diverting it all to the anxious individual and his or her stressors or fears. Anxiety also brings many irrational fears such as jealousy, fear of commitment, and unrealistic expectations. OCD and panic disorders have been associated with sexual dysfunction in women (Minnen & Kampman, 2000), and significant sexual difficulties for men (Letourneau, Schewe, & Frueh, 1997). Agoraphobia has been associated with greater criticism and less positive problem-solving interactions (Chambless et al., 2002).

Depression and marital distress are commonly co-occurring (Whisman, 1999). This mental health disorder been associated with negative behaviors: less problem solving capabilities (Johnson & Jacob 1997), decreased libido (Uebelacker & Whisman, 2005), attributing the negative partner's behavior to global causes or associations (Fincham & Bradbury 1993), power struggles, greater inequality, and distress with how partners make decisions in their relationships (Whisman & Jacobson, 1989), as well as depressed partners noting fewer positive and more negative interactions with their partners (Zlotnick, Kohn, Keitner, & Grottta, 2000). A depressed person may cause their partner to feel burdened, ambivalent, and silently resentful (Gupta & Beach, 2003), feelings that may or may not be noticeable.

Substance abuse has been associated with less positive communication, more struggles for control, avoidance of taking responsibility (denial), and verbal abusiveness (Fals-Stewart & Birchler 1998), as well as sexual problems among some alcoholic men (O'Farrell 1990).

Without a doubt, the existence of mental health disorders can create a more complex picture in the difficulty of relationships, given that the symptoms of mental health disorders can increase negative interactions, conflicts, and disagreements in couples. The treatment of mental health disorders is key for the success of a relationship given that untreated disorders can make it more difficult for partners to relate to one another. If you or your partner struggle with a mental health disorder, you both may want to consider receiving treatment from a psychiatrist, mental health counselor, or a psychologist. You can seek treatment yourself, or you can talk to your primary doctor about your symptoms and he or she can make a recommendation for further treatment.

Sally and Albert were two successful professionals who jointly owned a business. They had been married for ten years and had three children together. They came to therapy after Sally's dad passed away. Shortly after this Albert discovered that Sally was having a "platonic" relationship with a staff member of the hospital whom she had met when her dad had been under treatment the previous year. Albert had difficulty trusting and suffered from anxiety. Sally was not fully invested in the relationship because she refused to end the platonic relationship she had. She also struggled to communicate her needs in the relationship, leaving Albert guessing. During the therapy it was suggested that Albert seeks individual treatment for his anxiety and that Sally seeks individual treatment to discuss the root of her refusal to end this platonic relationship. The couple suddenly stopped coming to therapy and everything was left in the air. After six months Sally expressed her interest in receiving individual therapy. During the six months she was absent, the couple decided to separate, and each one had their own place. Albert was still not receiving treatment for his anxiety, and Sally continued to refuse to end her platonic relationship. During my individual work with Sally, she was served with divorce papers. It took a while for Sally to realize that her actions had made it difficult for Albert to recover trust, and that her hesitancy to end a platonic relationship had a costly impact in her relationship with her partner. Eventually, she also ended her platonic relationship since it no longer provided anything meaningful, but insecurity and self-doubt. Sally was able to accept her new reality and moved forward in life. Albert did not receive treatment for his anxiety, which will most likely continue to affect his future relationships.

All relationships don't have to work, and only you can make the decision to commit to your relationship. Even if you commit, there are no guarantees that the person that you're in a relationship with is the person for you, or is equally committed. If you're not sure if you want to be in this relationship, take some time to think about your decision. Try to avoid making impulsive decisions about the future of your relationship, otherwise you may be perceived as undecided and confused by your partner. Balance the good times and the bad times— all relationships have difficulties and struggles, and not everything is perfect. At times the grass is greener in your neighbor's yard, but you are not the one doing the mowing, and do not know how much it takes to have it looking so good.

If the aforementioned issues addressed in this chapter are identified and worked on, relationships can endure, and be filled with love and joy. Couples can try to solve these issues on their own and be successful, and this book covers many concepts, ideas, and suggestions to help you work on these problems. However, if you try on your own with the help of this and other books unsuccessfully, maybe it's time to consider professional help. Many of these factors are difficult to resolve even with professional help. Therapy can be a difficult process for many, and sometimes things can get worse before they get better. It requires effort, commitment, time, and money. More importantly, therapy can also be a place where feelings are brought to the surface, but it can also be a place where new, more positive behaviors can be learned, where compromises can be made, and alternative solutions can be found.

CONCLUSION

I hope that reading this book can shine some light onto your relationship problems, but more importantly that it has given you some tools and techniques to do something about these issues. Our relationships can be a source of stress and suffering if they're not working. With all of the external stressors that we have no control of, you can at least exert some influence over your own relationship and change it for the better.

ABOUT THE AUTHOR

 Ana Aluisy is a Licensed Marriage and Family Therapist and Mental Health Counselor in Tampa, Florida. She specializes in working with multicultural relationships, by helping individuals from different cultural backgrounds create healthy relationships filled with trust and understanding. Ana is the President of the Suncoast Mental Health Counselors Association and has been featured as an expert on TV, radio, newspapers, magazines, and blogs. Ana has worked with couples and families for close to ten years. During that time she has helped hundreds of individuals and couples improve their relationships.

Ana is also a veteran of the United States Marine Corps, she completed her Bachelor's degree in Psychology while in active duty and later finished a Master's degree in Rehabilitation and Mental Health Counseling.

Ana lives in Tampa Florida with her husband and sons. She is passionate about learning and helping individuals thrive in their relationships. You can follow her @AnaAluisy.

REFERENCES

2008 Physical Activity Guidelines for Americans. (2008). Retrieved July 13, 2014, from http://www.health.gov/paguidelines

Allemand, M., Amberg, I., Zimprich, D., & Fincham, F. (2007). The Role of Trait Forgiveness and Relationship Satisfaction in Episodic Forgiveness. *Journal of Social and Clinical Psychology, 26*(2), 199-217. Retrieved December 3, 2014.

Amato, P. R., & Rogers, S. J. (1997). A longitudinal study of marital problems and subsequent divorce. *Journal of Marriage and the Family, 59*, 612–624. Retrieved September 12, 14.

American Psychological Association. *Forgiveness: A Sampling of Research Results.* (2006). Retrieved July 2, 2014 http://www.apa.org/international/resources/forgiveness.pdf

Atwood, J.D., & Schwartz, L. (2002). Cybersex: The new affair treatment consideration. *Journal of Couple and Relationship Therapy, 1*(3), 37-56.

Bargh, J. (1990). Auto-motives: Pre-conscious determinants of thoughts and behavior. In E. Higgins & R. Sorrentino (Eds.), *Handbook of motivation and cognition: Foundations of social behavior.* (Vol. 2, pp. 93-130). New York: Guilford Press.

Beck, A. (1989). Reinforcing the Foundations. In *Love is never enough: How couples can overcome misunderstandings, resolve conflicts, and solve relationship problems through cognitive therapy.* New York: Perennial Library.

Beck, A. (2005). The Current State Of Cognitive Therapy: A 40-Year Retrospective. *Archives of General Psychiatry, 62,* 953-959.

Boundary. (n.d.). Retrieved October 1, 2014, from http://www.merriam-webster.com/dictionary/boundary

Bowlby, J. (1958) The nature of the Child's tie to his mother. *International Journal of Psychoanalysis, 39,* 350-373.

Bowlby, J, (1969) *Attachment and loss: Vol. I: Attachment.* New York: Basic Books.

Bowlby, J, (1973) *Attachment and loss: Vol. Ii: Separation, anxiety, and anger.* New York: Basic Books.

Bowlby, J, (1980) *Attachment and loss: Vol. III: Loss, sadness and depression.* London: Hogarth.

Bradford, K. (2012). Assessing Readiness For Couple Therapy: The Stages Of Relationship Change Questionnaire. *Journal of Marital and Family Therapy, 38,* 486-501. Retrieved October 12, 2014, from Pub Med.

Brehm, J. (1999). The Intensity of Emotion. *Personality and Social Psychology Review,* (3), 2-22. Retrieved December 22, 2014.

Buss, D., & Shackelford, T. (1997). From Vigilance To Violence: Mate Retention Tactics In Married Couples. *Journal of Personality and Social Psychology, 72*(2), 346-361. Retrieved November 24, 2014.

Call, V., Sprecher, S., & Schwartz, P., (1995). The incidence and frequency of marital sex in a national sample. *Journal of Marriage and the Family, 57,* 639-652.

Cannon, W. (1967). *The wisdom of the body* ([Rev. and enl. ed.). New York: Norton.

Chambless, D., Fauerbach, J., Floyd, F., Wilson, K., Remen, A., & Renneberg, B. (2002). Marital interaction of agoraphobic women: A controlled, behavioral observation study. *Journal of Abnormal Psychology, 111,* 502-512.

Chapman, G., & Chapman, G. (2007). *The heart of the five love languages.* Chicago: Northfield Publ.

Chapman, G. (2010). *The 5 love languages: The secret to love that lasts.* Chicago: Northfield Pub.

Christopher, F., & Sprecher, S. (2000). Sexuality In Marriage, Dating, And Other Relationships: A Decade Review. *Journal of Marriage and Family, 62,* 999-1017. Retrieved November 25, 2014.

Contempt. (n.d.). Retrieved July 17, 2014, from www.merriam-webster.com/dictionary/contempt

Cooper, M., Barber, L., Zhaoyang, R., & Talley, A. (2011). Motivational pursuits in the context of human sexual relationships. *Journal of Personality, 79,* 1031-1066.

Davidson, J., Darling, C., & Norton, L. (1995). Religiosity and the sexuality of women: Sexual behavior and sexual satisfaction revisited. *Journal of Sex Research, 32,* 235-243. Retrieved November 25, 2014.

De Judicibus, M., & Mccabe, M. (2002). Psychological factors and the sexuality of pregnant and postpartum women. *Journal of Sex Research, 39,* 94-103. Retrieved November 25, 2014.

Donnelly, D. (1993). Sexually inactive marriages. *Journal of Sex Research, 30,* 171-179. Retrieved November 25, 2014.

Donnelly, D., & Burgess, E. (2008). The Decision to Remain in an Involuntarily Celibate Relationship. *Journal of Marriage and Family, 70*(2), 519-535.

Donnelly, D., Burgess, E., Anderson, S., Davis, R., & Dillard, J. (2001). Involuntary celibacy: A life course analysis. *Journal of Sex Research, 38*(2), 159-169. Retrieved November 24, 2014.

Edwards, J., & Booth, A. (1994). Sexuality, marriage, and well-being: The middle years. In A. Rossi (Ed.), *Sexuality across the life course.* Chicago: University of Chicago Press.

Ekman P. (1984). Expression and the nature to emotions. Retrieved August 14, 2014 http://www.paulekman.com/wp-content/uploads/2013/07/Expression-And-The-Nature-Of-Emotion.pdf

Fals-Stewart, W., & Birchler, G. (1998). Marital interactions of drug-abusing patients and their partners: Comparisons with distressed couples and relationship to drug-using behavior. *Psychology of Addictive Behaviors, 12*, 28-38.

Fincham, F., Beach, S., & Davila, J. (2004). Forgiveness And Conflict Resolution In Marriage. *Journal of Family Psychology,* 72-81. Retrieved June 2, 2014.

Fincham, F., & Bradbury, T. (1993). Marital Satisfaction, Depression, And Attributions: A Longitudinal Analysis. *Journal of Personality and Social Psychology, 64*, 442-452.

Fisher, H. (1998). Lust, Attraction, And Attachment In Mammalian Reproduction. *Human Nature, 9*(1), 23-52.

Fisher, H. (2005). Web of Love: Lust, Romance and Attachment. In *Why we love: The nature and chemistry of romantic love.* New York: Henry Holt and.

Fisher, H. (2006). The Drive to Love: The Neural Mechanism for Mate Selection. In R. Sternberg & K. Sternberg (Eds.), *The new psychology of love* (pp. 87-110). New Haven, CT: Yale University Press.

Fisher, H. (2010, January 1). Real Aphrodisiacs to Boost Desire. *O, The Oprah Magazine*.

Fotopoulou, A., & Fisher, H. (2012). Generalized brain arousal mechanisms and other biological, environmental, and psychological mechanisms that contribute to libido. In *From the couch to the lab: Trends in psychodynamic neuroscience* (pp. 67-84). Oxford: Oxford University Press.

Fraley, R. (2010, January 1). A Brief Overview of Adult Attachment Theory and Research | R. Chris Fraley. Retrieved September 9, 2014, from http://internal.psychology.illinois.edu/~rcfraley/attachment.htm

Fruzzetti, A.E., and K.M. Iverson. 2004. Mindfulness, acceptance, validation and "individual" psychopathology in couples. In *Mindfulness and Acceptance: Expanding the Cognitive-Behavioral Traditions*, ed. S. C. Hayes, V. M. Follette, and M. M. Linehan, 168-191. New York: Guilford Press.

Fruzzetti, A.E. 2006. *The High Conflict Couple: A dialectical behavior therapy guide to finding peace, intimacy & validation.* 93-140. New York: Guilford Press.

Gagnon, J. (1990). The Explicit and Implicit Use of the Scripting Perspective in Sex Research. *Annual Review of Sex Research, 1*(5). Retrieved November 24, 2014.

Gerhardt, P. (1999, March 30). The Emotional Cost of Infidelity; Family therapists examine the psychological roots of extramarital affairs. *The Washington Post*. Retrieved September 30, 2014, from http://www.washingtonpost.com/wp-srv/national/health/march99/infid033099.htm

Glass, S., & Staeheli, J. (2004). *Not "just friends": Rebuilding trust and recovering your sanity after infidelity.* New York: Free Press.

Goleman, D. (2005). *Emotional intelligence: Why it can matter more than IQ.* New York: Bantam Books.

Gordon, T. (2000). *Parent effectiveness training: The proven program for raising responsible children.* New York: Three Rivers Press.

Greenber, L,; Johnson S, (1998) *Emotionally Focused Therapy for Couples.* New York: The Guildford Press p. 67

Gottman, J. M. (1999). *The Marriage Clinic.* New York: Norton.

Gottman, J. M. (2011). *The science of trust: Emotional attunement for couples.* New York: W.W. Norton.

Gottman, J., Gottman, J., & Declaire, J. (2007). *Ten lessons to transform your marriage: America's love lab experts share their strategies for strengthening your relationship.* New York: Three Rivers Press.

Gottman, J., & Silver, N. (1999). How I Predict Divorce. In *The seven principles for making marriage work: A practical guide from the country's foremost relationship expert.* New York, NY: Three Rivers Press.

Gupta, M., & Beach, S. (2003). Depression. In D. Snyder & M. Whisman (Eds.), *Treating difficult couples: Helping clients with coexisting mental and relationship disorders* (pp. 88-113). New York: Guilford Press.

Halper, J. (1988). *Quiet desperation: The truth about successful men.* New York, NY: Warner Books.

Hassebrauk, M., & Fehr, B. (2002). Dimensions of relationship quality. *Personal Relationships*, 9, 253-270. Retrieved October 12, 2014, from http://onlinelibrary.wiley.com/store/10.1111/1475-6811.00017/asset/1475-6811.00017.pdf?v=1&t=i194fa3x&s=a0b91328185 af6d327c7d8a66aa42bba41ff75e5&systemMessage=Wiley+Online+Library+will+be+disrupted+on+the+18th+October+from+10%3A00+BST+%2805%3A00+EDT%29+for+essential+maintenance+for+approximately+two+hours+as+we+make+upgrades+to+improve+our+services+to+you

Hazan, C., & Shaver, P. (1987). Romantic love conceptualized as an attachment process. *Journal of Personality and Social Psychology*, 511-524. Retrieved July 9, 2014 http://www2.psych.ubc. ca/~schaller/Psyc591Readings/HazanShaver1987.pdf.

Hazan, C., & Shaver, P. (1990). Love and work: An attachment theoretical perspective. *Journal of Personality and Social Psychology*, 270-280.

Hazan, C., & Shaver, P. (1990). Attachment as an organisational framework for research on close relationships. *Psychological Inquiry*, 1-22.

Hibbs, B., & Getzen, K. (2009). *Try to see it my way: Being fair in love and marriage.* New York: Avery.

Impett, E., Peplau, L., & Gable, S., (2005) Approach and avoidance sexual motivation: Implications for personal and interpersonal well-being. *Personal Relationships, 12*, 465-482.

Johnson, S., & Jacob, T. (1997). Marital interactions of depressed men and women. *Journal of Consulting and Clinical Psychology, 65*, 15-23.

Jongsma, A. (2007). *Adult psychotherapy homework planner* (Second ed.).

Kahr, B. (2008). *Sex and the psyche: The truth about our most secret fantasies.* London: Penguin.

LaCoursiere, J. (2008). *Stages of Relationship Change and Individual and Couple Adjustment.* Unpublished master's thesis, University of Kentucky, Kentucky. Retrieved October 11, 2014, from http://uknowledge.uky.edu/gradschool_theses/521

LaRossa, R., and Reitzes, D., (1993). Symbolic Interactionism and Family Studies. In *Sourcebook of Family Theories and Methods: A Contextual Approach,* ed. P. Boss, W. Doherty, R. LaRossa, W. Schumm, and S. Steinmetz. New York: Plenum.

Lawler, K., Younger, J., Piferi, R., Jobe, R., Edmondson, K., & Jones, W. (2005). The Unique Effects Of Forgiveness On Health: An Exploration Of Pathways. *Journal of Behavioral Medicine, 28*(2), 157-167. Retrieved December 3, 2014.

Levenson, R., & Gottman, J. (1985). Physiological and affective predictors of change in relationship satisfaction. *Journal of Personality and Social Psychology, 49,* 85-94.

Lightfoot, C. (2013, March 19). A Collection of Affair Statistics. Retrieved September 30, 2014, from http://www.move-beyond-the-affair.com/blog/2013/03/19/a-collection-of-affair-statistics

Linehan, M. (1993). Emotion Regulation Skills. In *Skills training manual for treating borderline personality disorder.* New York: Guilford Press.

Linehan, M. (1993). Interpersonal Effectiveness Skills. In *Skills training manual for treating borderline personality disorder.* New York: Guilford Press.

MacDonald, L. (2010). *How to help your spouse heal from your affair: A compact manual for the unfaithful.* Gig Harbor, WA: Healing Counsel Press.

Marchand, J., & Hock, E. (2000). Avoidance And Attacking Conflict-Resolution Strategies Among Married Couples: Relations To Depressive Symptoms And Marital Satisfaction. *Family Relations, 49,* 201-206.

Maslow, A., & Frager, R. (1987). *Motivation and personality* (3rd ed.). New York: Harper and Row.

Miller, R., Yorgason, J., Sandberg, J., & White, M. (2003). Problems That Couples Bring To Therapy: A View Across the Family Life Cycle*. *The American Journal of Family Therapy, 31,* 395-407.

Muise, A., Impett, E., & Desmarais, S. (2013). Getting It On Versus Getting It Over With: Sexual Motivation, Desire, and Satisfaction in Intimate Bonds. *Personality and Social Psychology Bulletin, 39*, 1320-1332. Retrieved November 24, 2014.

Nezu, A., & Carnevale, G. (1987). Interpersonal problem solving and coping reactions of Vietnam veterans with posttraumatic stress disorder. *Journal of Abnormal Psychology, 96*, 155-157.

O'Farrell, T. (1990). Sexual functioning of male alcoholics. In Collins R., Leonard, K., & Searles J., (Eds.), *Alcohol and the family: Research and clinical perspectives* (pp. 244-271). New York: Guilford Press.

O'Leary, C. (1999). Themes in Family Therapy. In *Counselling Couples and Families a Person-Centred Approach*. London: SAGE Publications.

Ortigue, S., Bianchi-Demicheli, F., Patel, N., Frum, C., & Lewis, J. (2010). Neuroimaging Of Love: FMRI Meta-Analysis Evidence Toward New Perspectives In Sexual Medicine. *The Journal of Sexual Medicine, 7*(11), 3541-3552. Retrieved December 14, 2014.

Perel, E. (2006). *Mating in captivity: Reconciling the erotic and the domestic*. New York: HarperCollins.

Prochaska, J., & Diclemente, C. (1983). Stages and processes of self-change of smoking: Toward an integrative model of change. *Journal of Consulting and Clinical Psychology, 51*, 390-395. Retrieved October 12, 2014, from http://www.uri.edu/research/cprc/Publications/PDFs/ByTitle/Stages and Processes of self change.pdf

Prochaska, J., DiClemente, C., & Norcross, J. (1992). In Search Of How People Change: Applications To Addictive Behaviors. *American Psychologist, 47*, 1102-1114.

Prochaska, J., & Velicer, W. (1997). The Transtheoretical Model of Health Behavior Change.*American Journal of Health Promotion*, 38-48. Retrieved August 6, 2014 from http://www.uri.edu/research/cprc/Publications/PDFs/ByTitle/The%20

Transtheoretical%20model%20of%20Health%20behavior%20 change.pdf.

Schmitt, G., & Neubeck, G. (1985). Diabetes, Sexuality, and Family Functioning. *Family Relations, 34*, 109-109. Retrieved November 25, 2014.

Schneider, W. (2003). *Transtheoretical model of change with couples.* Doctoral

dissertation, Texas A&M University, Texas. Retrieved October 11, 2014

Sprecher, S. (2001). Equity And Social Exchange In Dating Couples: Associations With Satisfaction, Commitment, And Stability. *Journal of Marriage and Family, 63*, 599-613.

Sprecher, S. (2002). Sexual satisfaction in premarital relationships: Associations with satisfaction, love, commitment, and stability. *Journal of Sex Research, 39*(3), 190-196.

Staheli, L. (1998). *"Affair-proof" your marriage: Understanding, preventing and surviving an affair.* New York: Cliff Street Books.

Storaasli, R., & Markman, H. (1990). Relationship problems in the early stages of marriage: A longitudinal investigation. *Journal of Family Psychology, 4*, 80-98.

Trust. (n.d.). Retrieved September 9, 2014, from http://www.merriam-webster.com/dictionary/trust

Uebelacker, L., & Whisman, M. (2005). Relationship Beliefs, Attributions, and Partner Behaviors Among Depressed Married Women. *Cognitive Therapy and Research, 29*, 143-154.

Vaughan, P. (2003). *The monogamy myth: A new understanding of affairs and how to survive them.* New York: Newmarket Press.

Waite, L., Browning, D., Doherty, W., Gallagher, M., Luo, Y., & Stanley S. (2002). *Does Divorce Make People Happy? Findings from a Study of Unhappy Marriages,* New York: Institute of American Values.

What Respect Really Means in a Relationship. (n.d.). Retrieved
   October 1, 2014, from http://www.twoofus.org/educational-
   content/articles/what-respect-really-means-in-a-relationship/index.
   aspx

Whisman, M., & Jacobson, N. (1989). Depression, Marital
   Satisfaction, And Marital And Personality Measures Of Sex Roles.
   Journal of Marital and Family Therapy, 15(2), 177-186.

Whisman, M., Dixon, A., & Johnson, B. (1997). Therapists'
   perspectives of couple problems and treatment issues in couple
   therapy. *Journal of Family Psychology, 11*, 361-366.

Whisman, M. (1999). Marital Dissatisfaction And Psychiatric
   Disorders: Results From The National Comorbidity Survey.
   Journal of Abnormal Psychology, 108, 701-706.

Whisman, M. (2001). Marital adjustment and outcome following
   treatments for depression. *Journal of Consulting and Clinical
   Psychology, 69*, 125-129.

Wieselquist, J., Rusbult, C., Foster, C., & Agnew, C. (1999).
   Commitment, pro-relationship behavior, and trust in close
   relationships. *Journal of Personality and Social Psychology, 77*(5),
   942-966. Retrieved December 9, 2014.

Worthington, E. (2005). *Handbook of forgiveness*. New York:
   Routledge.

Worthington, E., Witvliet, C., Pietrini, P., & Miller, A. (2007).
   Forgiveness, Health, And Well-Being: A Review Of Evidence
   For Emotional Versus Decisional Forgiveness, Dispositional
   Forgivingness, And Reduced Unforgiveness. *Journal of Behavioral
   Medicine, 30*(4), 291-302. Retrieved December 3, 2014.

Wright, E., Wright, D., Perry, B., & Foote-Ardah, C. (2007). Stigma
   And The Sexual Isolation Of People With Serious Mental Illness.
   Social Problems, 54, 78-98. Retrieved November 25, 2014.

www.menstuff.org/issues/byissue/infidelitystats.html

www.infidelityfacts.com/infidelity-statistics.html

Zeigarnik, B. (1927). Uber das Behalten yon erledigten und underledigten Handlungen. Psychologische Forschung, 9, 1-85.

Zlotnick, C., Kohn, R., Keitner, G., & Grotta, S. (2000). The relationship between quality of interpersonal relationships and major depressive disorder: Findings from the National Comorbidity Survey. *Journal of Affective Disorders, 59*, 205-215.